A Guide to the Orchids of Bruce and Grey Counties, Ontario

Bruce-Grey Plant Committee
(Owen Sound Field Naturalists)

Colour Pictures by Dr. Donald R. Gunn
Courtesy of the Royal Botanical Gardens, Hamilton

3rd Reprint with revisions 2005

Stan Brown Printers Limited
Owen Sound, Ontario

Dedicated to the memory of the late Dr. Donald R. Gunn.
Nature enthusiast and orchid photographer par excellence.

ISBN 0-9680279-1-1

3rd Reprint with revisions 2005

Canadian Cataloguing in Publication Data

Main entry under title:

A guide to the orchids of Bruce and Grey
 Counties, Ontario

Includes bibliographical references and index.
ISBN 0-9680279-1-1

1. Orchids – Ontario – Bruce (County) –
Identification. 2. Orchids – Ontario –
Grey (County) – Identification. I. Owen
Sound Field Naturalists. Bruce-Grey Plant
Committee.

QK495.064G85 1997   584'.4'0971321   C97-930758-9

Other publications by the Bruce-Grey plant committee available from the Owen Sound Field Naturalists:
A Checklist of Vascular Plants for Bruce and Grey Counties, Ontario, 3rd Edition 2003
The Ferns of Grey and Bruce Counties, Ontario, 1999
The Asters, Goldenrods and Fleabanes of Grey and Bruce Counties, Ontario, 2000
Rare & Endangered Species of Grey and Bruce Counties, Ontario, 2001
The Geology and Land Forms of Grey and Bruce Counties, 2004

All books available from:
    The Bruce-Grey Plant Committee
    c/o The Owen Sound Field Naturalists
    Box 401, Owen Sound, Ontario N4K 5P7

Guides may also be obtained from:
    The Toronto Field Naturalists
    2 Carlton Street, No. 1519
    Toronto, Ontario M5B 1J3
    Telephone: 416-593-2656
    Office open Fridays 9:00 a.m. to 12:00 noon

Table of Contents

PREFACE iv
Acknowledgements v
Map of Bruce & Grey Counties vi
INTRODUCTION 1
   Bruce and Grey Counties 1
   Discovering Orchids 3
   Why Conservation 3
   The Orchid Family 4
      Flower Structure 5
      Pollination 6
      Reproduction and Growth 7
      Orchid Identification 8
ARTIFICIAL KEY to the ORCHIDS of BRUCE & GREY COUNTIES 10
ANNOTATED CHECKLIST OF THE ORCHIDS OF
BRUCE AND GREY COUNTIES 15
   Amerorchis 15
   Aplectrum 17
   Arethusa 19
   Calopogon 21
   Calypso 23
   Coeloglossum 25
   Corallorhiza 27
   Cypripedium 32
   Epipactis 39
   Galearis 41
Colour Plates 43-54
Table A: Climatic Zones of Bruce and Grey Counties 55
Table B: Chart of Approximate Flowering Times for The Orchids of
   Bruce and Grey Counties 56-57
Table C: Nationally and Provincially Rare Orchids of Bruce and Grey Counties 58
   Goodyera 59
   Liparis 64
   Listera 66
   Malaxis 70
   Piperia 73
   Platanthera 75
   Pogonia 88
   Spiranthes 90
Glossary 97
References 102
Index 104

Preface

This book has been developed as a field guide to the orchids of Bruce and Grey counties. These two counties combined are known to contain 46 orchid species, that is 77% of the species found in Ontario. The Bruce Peninsula alone has 44 of these species, more than are known from any other area of similar size in Ontario, possibly in North America. These two counties contain a wide range of habitats which, in turn, support a great variety of vascular plants. It is well known for the extraordinary diversity of both orchids and ferns, especially on the Bruce Peninsula. Bruce and Grey counties are located in the northern portion of southwestern Ontario. Almost triangular in shape, the area is bordered by Lake Huron on the west and Georgian Bay on the northeast. The area is approximately 8,367 square kilometres and includes 350 kilometres of the Niagara Escarpment with some of the most striking scenery in the province.

An illustrated description of each orchid species is given and there are details on flowering times, habitat requirements and distribution in this area and farther afield, as well as general information about the orchid family. The importance of conservation is emphasized. A simplified key is provided for identification. Orchids, like so many other living things which have attracted attention through the ages, have accumulated many names in several different languages. To avoid confusion, plant students and horticulturalists rely on the Latin (scientific) names which accord with internationally agreed rules. In this book the species are listed alphabetically by their Latin names. Many people find English names easier to deal with but these are not so reliable. They vary from one district to another or, sometimes, the same name is used for more than one species. However, English names, known to be in common use in this area, are included for each species. The sources for these names are listed in the references. The use of technical terms has been minimized as much as possible; those that do occur are found in the glossary.

Accurate identification of most plants relies primarily on the study of the flowers. However, many of our native orchids are either so small or so delicate that such a study could be damaging to the plant. In this book, the key and descriptions have been simplified to allow satisfactory identification "at arm's length" as far as possible. Diagrams for each species will assist in this process. Much of the information on each species relates directly to the Bruce-Grey area. Individual orchid enthusiasts can usefully contribute to local knowledge of these details by making careful observations, notes, photographs, drawings, etc, and communicating these to other naturalists and botanists, or to park staff if the location is within a national or provincial park.

Copies of this book can be obtained from:
The Bruce-Grey Plant Committee, c/o The Owen Sound Field Naturalists, Box 401, Owen Sound, ON N4K 5P7

Colour Plate Section between pages 43 and 54.
Pictures in the same order and number as the species list.

ACKNOWLEDGEMENTS

The Ministry of Natural Resources, Owen Sound Area Office, initiated this project in 1978 as a guide to the orchids of Cyprus Lake Provincial Park and the adjacent northern Bruce Peninsula. Several people were involved in the Ministry initiative: Joe Johnson and D. E. Renfrew – field work (1978); J. E. Thompson and L. Clarke – research; R. S. W. Bobbette and F. Westman – compilation and writing; R. J. Newell – sketches; Bob Gray – concept and co-ordination. Others who reviewed the original draft and made comments and suggestions were: P. M. Catling, Donald R. Gunn, A. Reddoch, J. Reddoch, A. A. Reznicek, and R. E. Whiting. The work remained as an unpublished report.

Creation of this current and expanded version was undertaken by the Bruce-Grey Plant Committee at the suggestion of Bob Gray and Nels Maher and with the co-operation of the Owen Sound Field Naturalists. Additional information on local variation and distribution was provided by Joe Johnson and recent Ministry of Natural Resources' Areas of Natural and Scientific Interest (A.N.S.I.) inventory reports. The following members have assisted with updating the original manuscript, proof reading and editing: Joan and Walter Crowe, Marg Gaviller, Bob Gray, Ellen and Orris Hull, Joe Johnson and Nels Maher. Joe Johnson, professional botanist, has added invaluable information garnered during decades of research in this area. Lenore Carrick was responsible for additional diagrams. Computerization of the text, research on additional species and writing of their descriptions, organizing illustrations and many other tasks were done by Doug Bulgin, a graduate student employed under the 1996 EYC program of the Ontario Ministry of Natural Resources. His hiring was organized by Lorraine Brown and Bob Gray. The Owen Sound M.N.R. office provided facilities and supervision and Walter Crowe assisted with administration. Coordination of the project was by Joan Crowe. John Lounds and John Riley of the Federation of Ontario Naturalists have given support and advice on publication.

Thanks are due to Ross Brown for allowing us to use his chart of flowering dates to which the late Dennis Rupert also made valuable contributions. This has been up-dated by Joe Johnson.

The Royal Botanical Gardens in Hamilton have generously made available pictures taken by the late Dr. Donald Gunn. Thanks are due to Dr. Chris Graham for facilitating access to the Gunn collection.

Financial assistance towards printing costs has come from the following:
The Owen Sound Field Naturalists
The Federation of Ontario Naturalists
The Saugeen Field Naturalists
Members of the Bruce-Grey Plant Committee

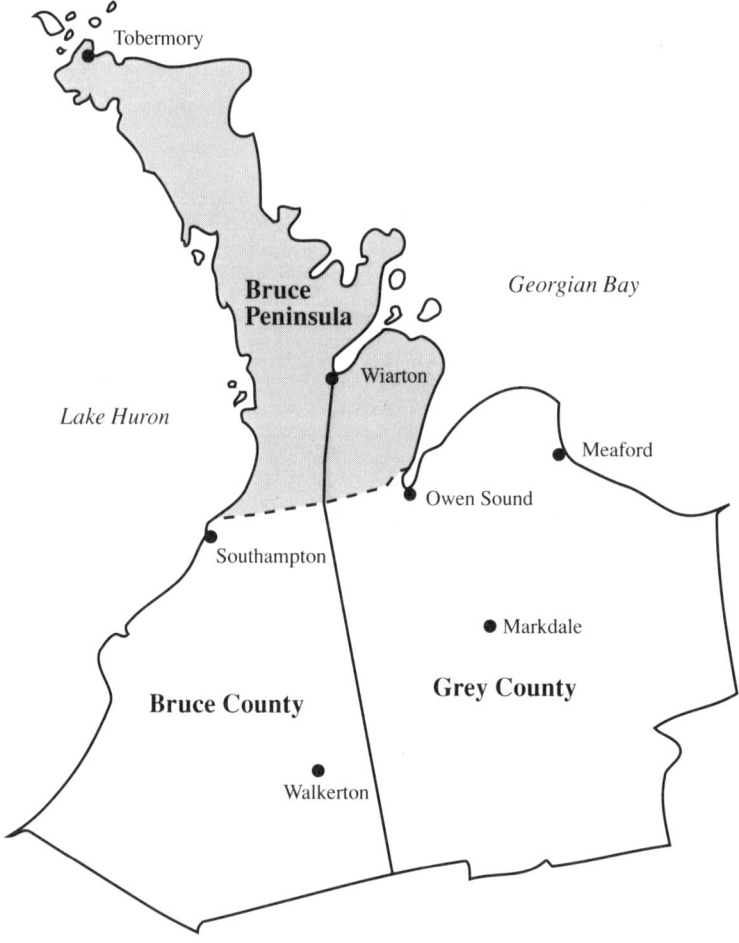

Figure 1: Bruce and Grey Counties – the Bruce Peninsula is north of the dotted line

INTRODUCTION

Bruce and Grey Counties

Bruce County is characterized by rolling pasture and cropland in the south and the rugged, still partially forested country of the Bruce Peninsula in the north. Grey County is a mosaic of woodlands, wetlands and agricultural land. The promontories and glens of the Niagara Escarpment run through it also, and it is overlain with an intricate web of cold-water streams and small inland lakes. Roughly triangular in shape, the two counties include approximately 750 kilometres of shoreline along Lake Huron and Georgian Bay. The Bruce Peninsula, which is a continuation of the Niagara Escarpment, serves to divide Georgian Bay from Lake Huron. With the exception of Keppel, Sarawak, and a small part of Derby Township in Grey County, the remainder of the peninsula is in Bruce County. It stretches like a thumb north and northwest from Highway 21, with the communities of Southampton and Owen Sound straddling its base. High cliffs of dolostone, which formed as coral reefs in the shallow, tropical seas of the Silurian period more than 400 million years ago, characterize the Georgian Bay side of the peninsula. The bedrock slopes gently westward to the low shelving rocks and sandy beaches of the Lake Huron side.

One of the last parts of southern Ontario to be settled, this region was essentially unexplored by white people until 1815, when Captain William Fitzwilliam Owen undertook a hydrographic survey of Georgian Bay and Lake Huron. However, little was known about the land, which was controlled by the Ojibway. In 1818, they turned over the easternmost part of Grey County to the Crown, but the major portion of the two counties (the so-called "Queen's Bush") was not surrendered by the Ojibway until 1836. European settlers began arriving by about 1840, and the area was soon dotted with communities and small farms. The Bruce Peninsula, except for some relatively small reserves, was given up by the natives in several stages between 1854 and 1885. In 1855, a railway from Toronto came to Collingwood, and by 1873 Owen Sound had a rail link to the south of the province. These lines led to greatly increased shipping on Georgian Bay, which in turn helped make the Bruce Peninsula more accessible. The Bruce Peninsula was thoroughly logged in the late 19th and early 20th centuries, but much of the land was found to be unsuitable for agriculture. Large town plots were laid out at Wiarton, Oliphant, Adair (Hope Bay), Hardwicke (Stokes Bay) and Bury (Tobermory). Only Wiarton achieved substantial growth. The Bruce Peninsula's long-established reputation as a wilderness was not seriously threatened until after 1945 when an influx of cottages took over many inland lakes and a substantial part of the shoreline, often in sensitive dune and fen areas which supported a unique assemblage of plants.

Glimpses of the botanical wealth of this area were first provided by the Canadian botanist, John Macoun, who collected plants here over one hundred years ago. More recently, an American, Professor M. L. Fernald, visited the Bruce Peninsula in the early 1920's, and described it as being a "place out of time." He supposed it to be the relict of past eons, having somehow survived the scourge of the last Ice Age. This idea was later challenged by geologists and botanists (Krotkov, 1940). It now seems evident that none of

Bruce or Grey Counties has been a glacial refugium. Modern studies also indicate that the northern two-thirds of the Peninsula as well as other parts near Lake Huron and Georgian Bay were covered by lake water derived from melting glaciers 11,000 to 12,000 years ago (Karrow, et al, 1975; Chapman and Putnam, 1966). The icy waters of post-glacial Lake Algonquin drained rather quickly (in geological terms) to low levels. A land bridge formed with Manitoulin Island to the northwest at a time (7,000 – 9,000 years ago) when Pine forests dominated the scene, and western vegetation expanded eastward (Bernabo and Webb, 1976). About 5,500 years ago, a new lake, Lake Nipissing, rose to drown the land bridge and even severed St. Edmunds and Lindsay townships from the Bruce-Grey mainland (Burden and McAndrews, 1973). Throughout the post-glacial period, changing water levels and a gradual rebounding of the earth's crust, due to the removal of the weight of glacial ice, brought about the present relationship of land and water.

Lake Huron and Georgian Bay with their prevailing westerly winds and on-shore breezes have an appreciable moderating effect on the climate of the twin counties. The cold water keeps air temperatures cool in the spring, normally retarding flowering until the danger of frost is past. In the autumn when the water is still relatively warm from the high air temperatures of summer, the lakes tend to keep the adjacent areas warmer, extending the local frost-free period. The lakes also provide a more than adequate moisture source for precipitation throughout the year. This moderating effect is one of the key reasons why the Meaford-Thornbury area of southern Georgian Bay, with an average of 140 frost free days, is the top apple producing region of the province. Inland, away from the moderating effects of the water, and with a considerable increase in altitude, the frost free days are fewer; for example, Durham has only 115. Thus, the climate throughout Bruce and Grey counties has considerable local variation (see Table A, page 55).

Such variations in climate may seem minor, but when combined with dramatically different shorelines from east to west, exposed uplands and sheltered valleys, and the contrast between rocky barrens, wetlands and woodlands, a great variety of microhabitats or "niches" is created. These are home to many native species of orchids as well as other flowering plants and non-flowering groups such as ferns, mosses, algae, fungi and lichens. The unique geological history and geographic location of the Bruce Peninsula have resulted in the occurrence of a striking combination of different plant species that have given the Bruce Peninsula its justified reputation as a botanical treasure-house. One of its major attractions has been the remarkable abundance of certain orchid species. The rest of Grey County, too, has part of the Niagara Escarpment while southern Bruce County has the fens and sandy shores of Lake Huron. Another feature of the west side of the peninsula is the phenomenon known as "cold bottom." This is caused by slow seepage of ground water from under deep sand dunes through relatively shallow sand. This keeps the ground cool in the summer and warm in the winter. In such areas water continues to move throughout the winter. "Cold bottom" may occur in other parts of our area for different reasons. These unusual conditions favour some orchid species. As well, in eastern North America, the climatic conditions found at a latitude of about 45 degrees seem to suit orchid species. It also seems that many orchids (as well as many ferns) respond well to calcareous conditions. These factors combine to make the two counties a very worthwhile destination for the botanical enthusiast. The nature of Bruce and Grey counties and their environment is so intricate and varied that we can only hope this brief outline will encourage readers to explore the area. Our emphasis is, of course, on the orchids, but whatever topic you choose, you will find that this area has a fascination all its own.

Discovering Orchids

Having decided to look for orchids, where should you begin? You may be lucky and find one in your own backyard, but most orchid species have very special habitat requirements. In order to see all the species in Bruce and Grey counties you will need to visit many locations with a variety of environmental conditions. When seeking orchids, a small group of two or three people is enough; larger groups tend to trample more plants than they can locate. It is wise to be discreet in telling of your finds. The beauty of these native wild flowers is enhanced by the thrill of personal discovery. Not everyone is to be trusted; many a prize colony has been eliminated by being revealed to greedy transplanters or thoughtless pickers. Orchids tend to die soon after transplanting because they are so habitat specific. For most orchids, successful transplanting requires that at least a "piece" of the local environment be moved with the orchid and that the habitat to which it is moved be carefully matched. This is an undertaking not to be approached lightly! Orchids wilt quickly when picked so they are unsuitable for flower arrangements and are much better enjoyed in their natural setting.

Why Conservation?

In North America we still need to learn to appreciate and conserve our remaining wilderness. The few hundred years of intense cultural expansion that we represent has not yet penetrated and put its stamp on every wild ravine or secluded swamp. The result is that we still have the chance to appreciate and understand wild environments, an opportunity denied to millions of people throughout the world. Population pressure is not strictly a human phenomenon. Many creatures besides people periodically undergo increases in numbers. However, it is no coincidence that, as our numbers increase dramatically, naturalists continually report the demise of communities and populations of animals and plants. In some cases, species disappear forever.

The orchids, as a group, experience exceptional destructive pressure from humans. The large scale collecting of wild plant specimens has been slowed in recent times, partly through legislation and partly through the commercial development of special seed germinating techniques. Nevertheless, collecting has not stopped in Ontario and wild stocks of our orchids are continually drained from the best known areas. However, today the most serious threat is land development with its destruction of natural vegetation and frequent manipulation of water levels. The only time that transplanting our native orchids should be attempted is when an area is doomed to destruction by highway construction, subdivision, etc.

A fine representation of scientific specimens from our study area is available in the collections of the Royal Ontario Museum Herbarium in Toronto and the Canadian Museum of Nature in Ottawa. The University of Guelph and the University of Waterloo as well as many herbaria in other parts of Canada and in universities in the northern United

States also hold specimens from this area. Many professional botanists have worked here, so these days almost no orchid specimen needs to be collected. Records are best made by photographs, descriptions, and sketches.

Of the forty-six species and two varieties of orchids found in Bruce and Grey counties, seven species and one variety are considered to be rare in Ontario (see Table C, page 58). One species, Small White Lady's Slipper (*Cypripedium candidum*), is listed as endangered for both Ontario and Canada. However, it is a historical record for Bruce County and there have been no confirmed reports from this area for over seventy years. Another species, Prairie Fringed Orchid (*Platanthera leucophaea*) is listed as vulnerable for both Ontario and Canada.

Statements about rarity are not always what they seem. For instance, a plant which is designated as "rare" in Ontario may be locally abundant. Thus, in a few bogs in this area, you will find that the rare White Fringed Orchis (*Platanthera blephariglottis*) is actually quite common. Plants that are not listed as rare because they are found over a wide geographic area may only occur in small, scattered populations. Whether growing in local areas of abundance, or in scattered populations, many of our orchids are still in a precarious position. Frivolous handfuls of plucked blossoms destroy the future of any population and thoughtless pickers soon bemoan "what used to be." Photographers, astonished at the mysterious beauty of some species, crush other "less impressive" mates around their focus of interest and may "garden" away "undesirable" companion plants or local features. This often alters the surrounding environment to the detriment of the very plant that they are so careful to highlight. Although it is important to protect individual specimens, the best way to preserve orchids is to preserve their habitats. The Province of Ontario and Canadian Heritage, Parks Canada recognize the basic importance of nature and the environment in their provincial and national parks. They have made it illegal to cut, remove or damage any plant or tree therein. What right have we to destroy what we cannot replace?

The Orchid Family

Orchids are considered to be the most evolutionarily advanced of all the flowering plants. No fossil record of them is known to exist. The ancient Chinese sage, Confucius, mentioned orchids as flowers of great refinement, to be held in high esteem. In ancient Greece, Theophrastus, a contemporary of Plato, was the first to use the name "orchis" for these plants and supposed some to have medicinal value. Since his time, orchids have had limited use as medicines, teas and food. Today, the only major commercial product is vanilla flavouring which is extracted from the seed pods of a tropical American species (*Vanilla planifolia*).

Most interest, and the main business in orchids, centres on their flowers, which are often colourful and beautiful, and always intriguing. Orchids grow from the tropics to well north of the Arctic Circle, and from sea level to 5,000 metres in elevation. The vast majority (80%) occur in tropical areas and many are epiphytic. It was not until the "dark continents" were penetrated in the late nineteenth century that the true immensity of the family came to light. The first species that was introduced into Europe for its beauty was the stately Showy Lady's Slipper (*Cypripedium reginae*) in 1641. Surprisingly, this plant is not some exotic from a steaming jungle, but can be found right here in Bruce and Grey counties.

Any group of plants which attracts a great deal of attention tends to be divided by taxonomists into many species. Estimates of as many as 35,000 orchid species world-wide reflect this, but the more probable number of 25,000-30,000 species is no less imposing. The orchids are one of the few really immense, and recently evolved, flowering plant families on the earth, yet nowhere do they dominate extensive areas of vegetation. Their dramatic beauty and curious forms are enhanced by their rarity.

Flower Structure

Peoples' natural curiosity about flowers has sparked the modern classification within which flowering plants are studied. For centuries botanical scholars throughout the world have uprooted, dismembered and studied flowering plants so that today we do not need to do this. It is sufficient for us to read and study diagrams and pictures in order to appreciate the whole flower as more than the sum of its parts, and to understand the living plant as it matures and sets the seeds of its future.

Two hundred years ago, the German poet Goethe suggested that all the parts of the flower (except the ovary and anther) are actually highly modified leaves. This rather startling idea can in fact be seen to be reasonable by anyone who spends a few years carefully observing plants. Thus, throughout the Plant Kingdom, leafy bracts grade into sepals, which grade into the showy, familiar flower petals. Even the stamens and pistil are derived from leaves. All of these flower parts tend to occur in consecutive circles or whorls. In lilies these whorls contain parts in groups of three. Their relatives, the orchids, have some dramatic modifications but three is still the basic number for petals and sepals. Orchid sepals are often similar to two of the petals in colour and/or shape but the third petal has changed to form a dramatically different "lip" or, in some cases, a "slipper."

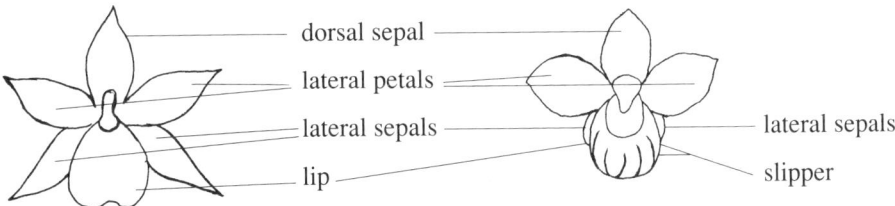

Fig. 2. Diagrams of flower showing petals, sepals and lip

Orchid blossoms are bilaterally symmetrical, which means that the flower can only be cut in one particular vertical plane in order that the right half of the flower will be a mirror image of the left. Radially symmetrical flowers on the other hand can be divided vertically along any plane to produce mirror images. Orchid stamens are fused with the pistil to form the distinctive column which is the reproductive centre of all orchid blossoms. In our species the flowers are "perfect," producing both pollen and seeds. The ovary is always inferior (below the perianth) and the fruit is a capsule in most species of orchid. Many species also have a spur which is an extension of the lip and contains nectar.

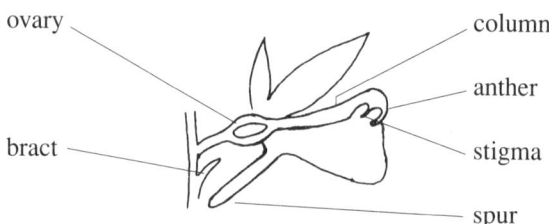

Fig. 3. Diagram of flower in section showing spur and column

Pollination

Until the early eighteenth century, it was not understood that pollen was essential to produce seeds. The various mechanisms for pollen transfer had not been worked out. Even as late as 1860, Darwin was a pioneer when he discussed the role insects play in the pollination of orchids. He argued that pollination of orchids and, in consequence, their floral structure are uniquely adapted to and symbiotic with insects. The floral structure of orchids and the specific insects pollinating them have evolved together.

Many plants can be self-pollinated. However, most of our orchids receive pollen on the stigma from a second plant in order to produce seeds and all of those normally require an insect to accomplish the transfer. In the course of evolution, the development of the orchid flower seems to have centred around the tempting, tricking, or rewarding of insects that assist in pollination. Like many flowers, orchids often produce nectar. This food is always associated with the lip, and it may exude from small glands or tubercles, or be contained in a short or long tubular spur that projects backwards from the lip (Figure 3). Colour, too, is often an attraction, alone or in combination with odour and distinctive shapes. The Prairie White Fringed Orchid (*Platanthera leucophaea*) becomes most fragrant at dusk and so attracts pollinating moths, which easily locate the pale white blossoms in he darkness and are treated to nectar as they probe the long spurred flower. Another strategy is employed by the Lady's Slippers (*Cypripedium* spp.). The "slipper" of these flowers is not necessarily fragrant, but it is always colourful and may hold a taste of nectar inside. Many a bee squeezes its way into this remarkable flower only to find retreat impossible! Three alternatives are presented: the bee may remain trapped and die; it may literally "eat its way out" through the pouch; or it may take advantage of two strategically located exits positioned at the back of the lip on either side of the column. The latter is the preferred choice and most commonly the course taken. Thus, the bee picks up pollen from the anther and transfers it to another flower.

It may seem as though orchids "bend over backwards" to provide for their insect pollinators. In almost every case, this is literally true! The lip of an orchid is actually the uppermost petal but, well before the plant comes into bloom, the ovary twists through 180 degrees so that the lip becomes the lowermost part of the flower. Grass pink (*Calopogon tuberosus*), with its lip clearly at the top of the flower, is the only exception in this area.

All of this remarkable attraction and guidance has one object: to place the insect in the proper position to first receive and then transfer the pollen. For example, in the case of the Prairie White Fringed Orchid, two adhesive pads of pollen stick to the tongue, eyes or head of the feeding insect. At first these will be erect, but after a short time they bend forward, so that when the insect probes another flower, the pollen will squarely strike the stigma and pollination will occur. In the Lady's Slipper, the insect simply brushes past the pollen masses on its way out "the back door." When this action is repeated in another flower, some of the pollen caught on its back is transferred to the stigma, just before the insect brushes past the left or right pollen masses of that second flower as it exits. One of the most interesting things to do when orchid hunting is to sit patiently near some plants and watch the various insects that may visit.

Reproduction and Growth

By the mid-nineteenth century, details of orchid pollination had been described but it required over fifty more years before the exacting requirements of orchid seed germination were clearly understood. As orchids were brought more and more into cultivation and the fame of their flowers spread, incessant attempts were made to propagate them. Very early on, it was observed that the tiny, dust-like orchid seeds are produced in prodigious numbers. Most of our native species have thousands of seeds per capsule but some tropical orchids produce more than four million seeds from each flower! It would seem that they have the potential to overrun the earth and yet they do not.

The reluctance of orchid seeds to germinate and grow in nature also occurred in the greenhouses of collectors, who had to resort to the pirating of wild plants in order to maintain and expand their stock. Out of the thousands of seeds sown, perhaps only a few dozen would germinate and even fewer mature. This situation continued until the 1920's, when experiments using a sterile nutrient growing medium unravelled the mystery. The rather complicated laboratory procedures used in this approach were no more complex than the actual process which takes place in nature (Correll, 1950).

Orchid seeds are so small that they can be dispersed by the wind. They are naked except for a frail net-like covering called the testa. They are similar to the germ of wheat but with only extremely limited food reserves. With almost no stored food, the tiny seed has nothing to "build with." Moreover, orchids are unique among the higher plants in not having an embryonic root. How then can this tiny speck grow into such a spectacular plant? The answer to this question is similar to that concerning orchid pollination – there is an intervening agent, a second symbiotic relationship. In nature, it seems that orchid seeds cannot grow successfully until invaded by a fungus. These fungi apparently act as the "digestive system" for the orchid cells and form a vital early link between the surrounding soil and the young plant. This allows the orchid to take up the food needed to develop first a protocorm with hair-like rootlets, then the single seed leaf characteristic of the monocotyledons and, finally, true roots.

Orchids grow as herbaceous perennials, and our native species either die back to ground level each year or, in a few cases, have overwintering leaves. Gradually, given the right habitat and freedom from natural enemies, the young orchid grows to maturity and blossoms after one to ten years, depending largely on the species. A few species require an even longer period before they flower. Finally, a seed is formed and the life cycle begins anew.

A few of our orchids never grow leaves but are indirectly saprophytic. They derive nutrients from associated fungi which extract them from the leaf mould of the forest floor. These have highly specialized coralloid root systems that give rise to the descriptive name, Coralroot Orchids (*Corallorhiza* spp.). They appear above the surface of the ground only when flowering and fruiting.

The presence of special symbiotic soil fungi is only one of the conditions necessary for orchid growth. Germination must occur under the proper conditions of soil, moisture, temperature and light if the plant is to flourish and continue. Many orchids have very precise requirements and only a few can thrive in diverse environments. By carefully reading the habitat description for each species, it is actually possible to predict some orchid locations by recognizing the conditions of vegetation and microenvironment favoured by that species.

Orchid Identification

It is easy for most people to see that the brilliant large-flowered Lady's Slippers (*Cypripedium* spp.) and Grass Pink (*Calopogon tuberosus*) are orchids, but most of our native species are much smaller and less colourful. Their kinship to the familiar tropical corsage flowers is often not readily observed.

For the beginner in the Bruce and Grey area, there are two sure ways to identify a plant as an orchid: either by the seed capsule or the flower. Seed capsules are one of the most certain ways of knowing you have an orchid. They always occur below the blossom and the flowering parts frequently remain attached, but shrivelled, at the tip of each fruit. They also shed their seeds, or dehisce, in a distinctive fashion. Rather than opening at one end or the other, or falling apart, orchid capsules split along their sides, like a tiny, elongated barrel with some of the staves missing. Through the slits left by the "missing staves," the tiny seeds are released. The dead fruit stalks of orchids often persist over the winter attached to the dormant underground parts. The dust-like nature of the seeds enables them to be dispersed by wind over a period of time and over great distances. However, they will only germinate if their landing site fulfils their exact habitat requirements.

Most people want to see orchids in bloom, so identification of species will usually be focused on flowers and other characteristics to be found at that time. If you see a plant you believe to be an orchid, or have a photograph, it is possible to identify it by means of a "key." When taking a photograph for later identification, details of the habitat, size of the plant and flower, presence or absence of leaves, etc. should be noted. Most photographs, however beautiful, do not show all the parts needed to identify the species.

A binary key is a series of descriptive statements giving two choices at each numbered stage. The plant to be identified will always be described by one of these statements better than the other. At the end of the chosen statement will be a number which leads to a second set of descriptions and through this process of elimination the name of the plant is finally reached. It is important to read both statements in each couplet before making your choice.

One of the easiest things to notice is whether or not the stem that holds the flower or raceme has leaves. Leaves should not be confused with bracts which are very reduced. On some species they intergrade. If we use this as a key feature, we have the following descriptive statements:

1a Flower, raceme or spike on a leafless stalk **or** leaves only at the base of the stalk.........2
1b Flower or raceme with one or several leaves on stalk. May also have basal leaves. 28

If the plant is best described by 1a go to the descriptions at 2a and 2b and choose between them. If 1b is selected go to 28a and 28b and choose again. The name of each species emerges progressively as the key "runs out." The first few choices in the key are usually quite clear-cut but further into the key it may seem that none of the features apply to the plant you are identifying. This may be due to one of the four following reasons:

1) A wrong choice has been made at an earlier point, and it is necessary to "back-track" to find the mistake.
2) Your specimen is not typical. Perhaps the colour or size, the number of flowers or leaves is unusual for that species. "Cast around" the key for the "best fit." Read the descriptions for each species in that group.
   Usually, by looking at all the features, it is possible to make a diagnosis.
3) You have found a rare orchid previously unknown in the area. In this case, follow the "best fit" through the key, and look at the description of the species you do arrive at. If this happens it will be necessary to consult an orchid flora which covers a wider geographic area in order to find a species close to your "best fit."
4) You have found a plant that resembles an orchid, but is not. Check again for the orchid lip, sepals and petals and the column within the flower. Also look for capsules and an ovary that is below the insertion of the petals. Make sure that the leaves have parallel veins.

Once the species is determined from the key, the description and illustration in the text may be checked for verification. The species description page number is given in the key. It is also wise to check the genus description in the text, located in front of the species descriptions. There is no "cheating" associated with using the key, so feel free to jump ahead to the orchid descriptions, look at the illustrations, test guesses and refer often to the glossary. As you successfully locate and identify more plants, start your own checklist and make notes and sketches.

ARTIFICIAL KEY to the ORCHIDS of BRUCE and GREY COUNTIES
At Flowering Time

1a Flower, raceme or spike on a leafless stalk or leaves only at the base of the stalk. 2
1b Flower, raceme or spike with one or several leaves on stalk. May also have basal leaves. 28
2a Leaves absent at time of flowering (withered remnants at base of stalk may be visible). 3
2b Basal leaf or leaves clearly present at time of flowering. 10
3a Flower large (3-5 cm), solitary, magenta-pink. Lip pendant, pinkish-white, streaked with purple and yellow. Three fringed ridges down centre.
Arethusa bulbosa – **Arethusa (page 20)**
3b Flowers smaller, numerous, in spikes or racemes. 4
4a Stalk with sheathing scales. 5
4b Stalk with no sheathing scales. 9
5a Plant greenish-yellow. Flower yellowish-green to greenish-yellow, lip white.
Corallorhiza trifida – **Early Coralroot (page 31)**
5b Stem yellow or reddish-purple. Lip white marked with violet, magenta, or purple spots or stripes. 6
6a Lip 3-lobed. 7
6b Lip not lobed. 8
7a Lip shorter than petals, 3-lobed, white spotted with violet. Sepals and petals yellowish-brown mixed with purple. No spur. Overall colour brownish.
Aplectrum hyemale – **Putty Root (page 18)**
7b Lip with two small lateral lobes, white with crimson spots. Sepals and petals spotted or stained magenta to crimson. Spur a distinct swelling near top of ovary. Usually reddish purple to brownish but may be greenish-yellow.
Corallorhiza maculata – **Spotted Coralroot (page 28)**
8a Sepals and petals arching forward, yellowish-white with purple margins and stripes. Lip off-white to flesh-coloured or pink with purple stripes, may be mostly purple. No spur.
Corallorhiza striata – **Striped Coralroot (page 30)**
8b Sepals and petals purplish, lip whitish with purple margins and purple spots. Spur tiny, attached to top of ovary. Plant small and late flowering.
Corallorhiza odontorhiza – **Autumn Coralroot (page 29)**
9a Flowers greenish or yellowish with a slightly up-curved spur, tiny and widely spaced in a wand-like raceme. (2 basal leaves which die during flowering).
Piperia unalascensis – **Alaska Orchid (page 74)**
9b Flowers white, often tubular and in a relatively continuous spiralling raceme.
Spiranthes spp. – Ladies' Tresses 23
10a Plant usually with one basal leaf. 11
10b Plant with two or more basal leaves. 14
11a Leaf narrow, grass-like. Showy magenta flowers on a few-flowered raceme. Lip erect at top of flower.
Calopogon tuberosus – **Grass Pink (page 22)**
11b Leaf broader, elliptic or ovate. 12

12a Flower solitary, conspicuous, purplish-pink.
Lip a small, brightly coloured pouch with an "apron."
Leaf plicate.
***Calypso bulbosa* – Calypso (page 24)**
12b Flowers in a raceme, smaller, leaves smooth. 13
13a Flowers greenish-white. Lip strap-like, projecting backwards.
Raceme lax, few flowered.
***Platanthera obtusata* – Blunt Leaf Rein Orchid (page 84)**
13b Flowers pale rose. Lip with three lobes, white with purple spots,
projecting outwards. Raceme with two to six flowers, in rare cases more.
***Amerorchis rotundifolia* – Small Round Leaved Orchis (page 16)**
14a Plant with two basal leaves. 15
14b Plant with a rosette of several basal leaves. Flowers in a spike. 19
15a Leaves plicate and ascending. Flower large and solitary with a prominent
pink pouch.
***Cypripedium acaule* – Pink Moccasin Flower (page 33)**
15b Leaves smooth with a midrib, not plicate. Flowers in a raceme or spike. 16
16a No spur. Leaves ascending as the plant flowers. 17
16b Spur present. Leaves flat or low arching as the plant flowers. 18
17a Leaves slightly folded. Small, pale yellowish flowers in a raceme.
***Liparis loeselii* – Loesel's Twayblade (page 65)**
17b Leaves not folded. Large flowers in a raceme, pale purple with a white pendant lip.
***Galearis spectabilis* – Showy Orchis (page 42)**
18a Stem usually with two or three small bracts. Leaves shiny. Flowers in a raceme,
lip blunt, whitish in colour and directed downward.
Spur long but blunt and more or less horizontal.
***Platanthera orbiculata* – Round Leaved Orchid (page 85)**
Plants with very large leaves and a very prominent spur are a separate variety
of this species:
***Platanthera orbiculata* var. *macrophylla* – Dinner Plate Orchid (page 86)**
18b Stem usually without bracts. Leaves not shiny. Flowers in a spike, greenish to
yellowish-green, lip tapering to a point and upcurved.
Spur tapering to a point and directed downward.
***Platanthera hookeri* – Hooker's Orchid (page 80)**
19a Leaves ovate, dark green, usually with white (silver) veins.
Flowers globose, greenish or whitish.
Goodyera spp. – Rattlesnake Plantains 20
19b Leaves lighter green, no white veins, shapes vary. Flowers not globose.
Spiranthes spp. – Ladies' Tresses 23
20a Leaves with a broad white central stripe, other veins not markedly white.
Spike one-sided.
***Goodyera oblongifolia* – Menzies' Rattlesnake Plantain (page 60)**
20b No clear midstripe, but other veins definitely white, giving a reticulate pattern.
Spike one-sided, cylindrical or spiral. 21
21a Stalk densely glandular-hairy. Spike cylindrical.
***Goodyera pubescens* – Downy Rattlesnake Plantain (page 61)**
21b Stalk not densely hairy. Spike one-sided. 22

22a Plants small, ± 5-10 cm. Spike short, about 1/3 the length of the stem, strongly one-sided. Leaves dark green with light silvery reticulation. Flowers greenish-white. Lip saccate with a recurved tip.
Goodyera repens – **Lesser Rattlesnake Plantain (page 62)**

22b Plants slightly larger, ± 10-15 cm. Spike half the length of the stem. Leaves bluish-green with light-green reticulation. Flowers whitish in a loose spiral. Lip only slightly saccate, the tip only slightly recurved.
Goodyera tesselata – **Checkered Rattlesnake Plantain (page 63)**

23a Inflorescence usually a long, rather loose spiral. Lower flowers of the inflorescence about 4-7 mm long. 24

23b Inflorescence usually densely flowered. Lower flowers of inflorescence about 8-11 mm long. 26

24a Shiny lanceolate basal leaves persisting after flowering. 1-2 bracts on stem. Flowers often dense on the spike. Lip with a bright yellow stripe. Blooms June – July.
Spiranthes lucida – **Shining Ladies' Tresses (page 94)**

24b Leaves not persisting after flowering. Leaves lanceolate, elliptic, ovate or round. 3-6 bracts on stem. Flowers generally loosely arranged. Lip either green or cream-coloured. Blooms in July or later. 25

25a Lateral sepals about 2.5 times as long as wide. Flowers uniformly pale cream-coloured. Lip cream to pale yellow. Blooms August – September.
Spiranthes casei – **Case's Ladies' Tresses (page 91)**

25b Lateral sepals about 3.5 times as long as wide. Flowers whitish with yellowish-green at base. Lip more or less pale green.
Blooms mid-July to August, sometimes later.
Spiranthes lacera – **Northern Slender Ladies' Tresses (page 93)**

26a Lateral sepals 3 mm or more wide towards the base, not spreading. Lip tends to be sharply constricted about 2/3 from base. Veins of the perianth parts prominent. Flowers white or cream.
Blooms mid July to early September, sometimes later.
Spiranthes romanzoffiana – **Hooded Ladies' Tresses (page 96)**

26b Lateral sepals 2-3 mm wide, spreading. Lip not constricted. Veins of perianth not prominent. 27

27a Leaves absent at flowering. Flowers white. Central portion of lip yellowish and thickened. Flowers strongly fragrant. Lateral sepals diverge or ascend from other floral parts. Blooms September to October.
Spiranthes magnicamporum – **Great Plains Ladies' Tresses (page 95)**

27b Leaves present or absent at time of flowering. Flowers white, with slightly less fragrance. Urn-shaped, lateral petals and dorsal sepal coming together, lateral sepals slightly spreading. Blooms late August – September (occasionally into October).
Spiranthes cernua – **Nodding Ladies' Tresses (page 92)**

28a Plants with one leaf part way up stem. Bracts may also be present. 29
28b Plants with at least two leaves on stem. 32

29a One narrowly elliptic leaf with a long stalk sheathing the stem. Flowers conspicuous, rose-pink, usually solitary, occasionally two on stalk. No spur.
Pogonia ophioglossoides – **Rose Pogonia (page 89)**

29b Leaf broader. Numerous flowers in a raceme. 30

30a One oblanceolate leaf near base, angling upwards. Flowers small with a long curved spur, greenish or whitish, in a loose raceme, ± 10 flowers.
Platanthera clavellata – **Club Spur Orchid (page 77)**
30b Flowers very tiny, in a raceme, usually more than 20 flowers. No spur. 31

31a Pedicels 2 to 3 times longer than flowers.
Raceme densely flowered and flat topped.
Malaxis unifolia – **Green Adder's Mouth (page 72)**
31b Pedicels approximately equal to flower length.
Raceme spindly, thin and tapering.
Malaxis monophyllos – **White Adder's Mouth (page 71)**

32a Plants with 2 opposite leaves part way up stem. 33
32b Plants with 2 or more alternate leaves up stem. 35

33a Stout and coarse, leaves ovate to elliptic. Raceme with 20-60 yellow-green flowers. Lip with a minute tooth in the angle of the lobes.
Listera ovata – **European Common Twayblade (page 69)**
33b Plants smaller, leaves heart-shaped or broad-ovate.
Raceme with 25 or fewer flowers. 34

34a Leaves heart-shaped. Flowers mauve, purple or green.
Lip distinctly two-pronged, cleft to the middle or beyond.
Listera cordata – **Heart Leaved Twayblade (page 68)**
34b Leaves broad-ovate. Flowers translucent, greenish-white. Lip broad at tip, shallowly notched.
Listera convallarioides – **Broad Lipped Twayblade (page 67)**

35a Leaves smooth, with a midrib. Not plicate. Flowers with a spur, subtended by bracts in a raceme or spike. 36
35b Leaves slightly plicate. No spur. 43

36a Bracts of lower flowers conspicuous, 2-3 times longer than the flowers.
Flowers in a spike. 37
36b Bracts of lower flowers shorter and less conspicuous.
Flowers in a raceme or spike. 38

37a Flowers greenish, less than 1 cm. Lip with up-curved margins.
Bracts about 3 times longer than flowers.
Coeloglossum viride – **Long Bracted Green Orchid (page 26)**
37b Flowers greenish to yellowish, about 7 mm long. Lip flat with a lump (tubercle) in centre. Bracts about twice length of flowers.
Platanthera flava – **Tubercled Orchid (page 79)**

38a Flowers with a distinctly fringed lip, usually 3-lobed. 39
38b Lip of flower not fringed or lobed. 42

39a Flowers rose-purple, approximately 1 cm long.
Lip divided into 3 wedge-shaped segments, fringed at edges. Fragrant.
Platanthera psycodes – **Small Purple Fringed Orchid (page 87)**
39b Flowers white or greenish-white. 40

40a Flowers pale yellow to greenish-white, about 1 cm long.
Lip deeply divided into 3 wedge-shaped segments with a
deep claw-like fringe.
Platanthera lacera – **Ragged Fringed Orchid (page 82)**
40b Flowers pure or creamy white. 41

41a Flowers faint creamy-white, about 2.5 cm long.
    Lip 3-lobed, central lobe large and wedge-shaped.
    Platanthera leucophaea – **Prairie Fringed Orchid (page 83)**
41b Flowers usually pure white, about 2 cm long.
    Lip oblong, fringed with short hairs.
    Platanthera blephariglottis – **White Fringed Orchis (page 76)**

42a Flowers white, less than 1 cm long, in a thick, tall raceme. Clove-scented.
    Platanthera dilatata – **Tall White Bog Orchid (page 78)**
42b Flowers greenish or yellow-green, less than 1 cm long, in a spike.
    Platanthera hyperborea – **Tall Northern Green Orchid (page 81)**

43a Flowers purple or green tinged, about 2 cm, tinged with purple in a many-flowered, long raceme with leafy bracts smaller than the flowers.
    Epipactis helleborine – **Helleborine (page 40)**
43b Flowers conspicuous, colourful, with a saccate lip – "slipper."
    Usually solitary or in pairs. 44

44a Slipper small, white with red veins, tapering to a conical projection from the base.
    Cypripedium arietinum – **Ram's Head Lady's Slipper (page 34)**
44b Pouch larger, not veined, may be suffused with colour. 45

45a Pouch bright yellow, lateral petals twisted and green-brown to purplish brown.
    Cypripedium calceolus – **Yellow Lady's Slipper**
    (page 35, for varieties see text)
45b Pouch white, pink or rose. 46

46a Pouch white outside, inside faintly striped with purple.
    Lateral petals and dorsal sepal brownish.
    Cypripedium candidum – **Small White Lady's Slipper (page 37)**
46b Pouch strongly suffused with red or rose, rarely all white.
    Dorsal sepal and lateral petals white.
    Cypripedium reginae – **Showy (Queen) Lady's Slipper (page 38)**

Annotated Species List
Of the Orchids of Bruce and Grey Counties

It should be noted that plant and flower sizes vary according to habitat conditions and flowering times vary with changes in climatic conditions. The dimensions and flowering periods given here relate as much as possible to the local conditions of Bruce and Grey. Some dimensions are local averages – often indicated ±.

Genus: *Amerorchis* Hultén

This genus was named recently and has only one species. The Latin name is a combination of "America," which indicates that this plant is only found in North America, and "orchis." The name orchis has interesting ramifications. It comes from the Greek word meaning "testicle" because of the pair of tuberous growths resembling testicles found among the roots of many orchids. At the time of the "Doctrine of Signatures" in medicine, it was thought that if part of a plant resembled a human organ, the plant could be used to cure diseases in that part of the body. The roots of an *Orchis* were, therefore, considered to be efficacious in treating sexual problems and were often prescribed as a cure for impotence. This theory has no truth in it whatsoever, and was rejected long ago.

1. Small Round Leaved Orchis

Amerorchis rotundifolia (Banks ex Pursh) Hultén [*Orchis rotundifolia*]
Small Round Leaved Orchis

The English name is simply translated from the Latin *rotundifolia*. This beautiful little orchid, so common in the northwest of the continent, is widespread but local in the east. It has been found in only two locations in our area, both on the Bruce Peninsula: one population in Keppel township is still extant, the other in St. Edmunds Township has disappeared. Though small, less than 25 cm tall here, this is an orchis of rare and delicate beauty. The fact that it has characteristics of both the former *Orchis* genus and also of the Rein Orchids (*Platanthera* spp.) determined that it should be placed in its own genus and it is, indeed, distinctive. At the top of a somewhat curving stem perches a flower spike of one to eight flowers which are white to pale mauve-pink. They seem to "hover like tiny butterflies" (Lewis J. Clark, 1973). The showy white lip, three-lobed and spotted or blotched with deep purple, first catches your eye. Above the lip, the lateral petals and dorsal sepal form a pink hood and, on either side, the white or pinkish sepals spread like wings. The whole flower is hardly wasp-sized but charming nonetheless. At the base of the plant, one roundish or egg-shaped leaf clasps the stem, yellow-green in colour with a dull sheen. The plant prefers cold northern forests and shaded bogs and swamps, with plants such as Showy Lady's Slipper (*Cypripedium reginae*), Heart Leaved Twayblade (*Listera cordata*) and Three Leaved False Solomon's Seal (*Maianthemum trifolium*) growing nearby. Its season of bloom is June into early July.

Description
Height ±15 cm.
Leaf solitary, clasping stem near the base, dull yellow-green,
    ovate-elliptic, 3-10 x ±5 cm.
Raceme with 1-8 or more flowers. Bracts lanceolate, 7-15 x 3-5 mm.
Flowers white to pale pink blotched and spotted with deep purple.
Sepals squared-elliptic to ovate-elliptic, 3-5 nerved, 6-10 x 3-4 mm.
Petals 2-3 nerved, 5-6 x 2-3 mm, ovate-oblong, broadly obtuse, oblique,
    forming a hood with the dorsal sepal.
Lip deeply 3-lobed, middle lobe ±8 x ±5 mm, spatulate to cuneate.
    Lateral lobes smaller, elliptic.
Column short, beneath the hood. Spur slender, curved, 5-6.5 mm long.
Flowers: June to early July.
Capsules ellipsoid, ±1.5 cm long.

Genus:
Aplectrum Nuttall

The name of this genus derives from the Greek word *plectron* meaning spur. The prefix "a" indicates the absence of a spur in these flowers. There are only two species, one found in eastern North America and the other in Japan.

2. Putty Root

Aplectrum hyemale (**Muhl. ex Willd.**) **Nutt.**
Putty Root, Adam and Eve

The Latin word *hyemalis* means "belonging to winter" and refers to the overwintering leaf which appears in autumn but withers away, either before flowering or as it commences, in the spring. This unusual strategy is adapted to the temperate deciduous forest found at this latitude. The green overwintering leaf takes advantage of the greater light levels available before the trees leaf out, and is able to generate food stores which will eventually provide energy for flowering and seed development. Both the English names refer to the corms. Their sticky consistency made them useful to early settlers for mending broken crockery. No doubt the aboriginal people were aware of their qualities well before this. Putty Root plants do not bloom every year but produce a new corm each year which remains attached to the original by a thin rhizome. It is the new corm which puts forth the flower stalk early in the spring before the leaves mature on the trees. Pairs of corms are often found which is the origin of the English name "Adam and Eve." This led to numerous superstitions about these plants and attempts to use them for medicinal purposes. The latter were founded more on fancy than on fact.

Putty Root grows in upland deciduous forests from southern Quebec to Minnesota, south to Georgia. The brownish yellow flowers do not stand out against the dead leaves of the forest floor, so this is not an easy plant to discover. At this stage, it is very reminiscent of *Corallorhiza* (pages 27-31), but the latter never produce leaves. It is easiest to spot in leaf, in autumn or early spring. It has, moreover, suffered from the depredations of early settlers and the destruction of the temperate forest, as well as by logging and development in more recent times. It is rare in Ontario and has been recorded in this area only from three locations in the central Bruce Peninsula. It does, however, occur in Simcoe County, so it could also be found in Grey County in rich, well drained, deciduous woodlands.

Description:
Height ±20 cm.
Leaf 1, basal, elliptic 10 x 4 cm, leaf stalk 2-3 cm. Dark green with whitish veins, plicate, gradually turning brown in late spring.
Flowers 5-10 in a loose raceme, scape with a few sheathing bracts.
Sepals and lateral petals ±1 cm, oblanceolate, purplish tipped with brown.
Lip obovate, ±1 cm, 3-lobed. Central lobe wide, white marked with purple.
Column elongate, flattened, with a terminal anther. No spur.
Flowers: June
Capsule drooping, ellipsoid, ribbed, 2 cm long.

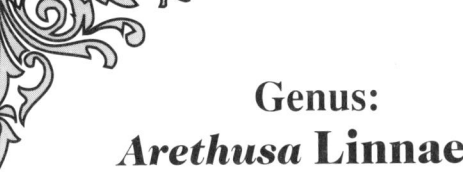

Genus:
Arethusa Linnaeus
Arethusa

The name of this genus comes from the Greek word "Arethusa." Arethusa was a nymph at the court of Artemis, goddess of chastity, the daughter of Zeus and the twin sister of Apollo. There are only two species, one in North America and one in Japan. The species name *bulbosa* refers to the bulbous corms which produce a single flower and a single, slender, smooth leaf blade after the flower fades. The early settlers in some areas used the corm as a remedy for toothache, with what success is not recorded!

3. Arethusa

Arethusa bulbosa L.
Arethusa, Dragon's Mouth, Swamp Pink

The colourful flowers make their brief appearance each spring in the cool bogs and fens usually growing deep in *Sphagnum*. The prominent lip has a crenulate edge and a colourfully fringed crest. The column bears a ventral anther with a pair of mealy pollinia. Arethusa can be found in the company of such plants as Rose Pogonia (*Pogonia ophioglossoides*), Grass Pink (*Calopogon tuberosus*), Sundews (*Drosera* spp.) and Pitcher Plant (*Sarracenia purpurea*), with the White Fringed Orchis (*Platanthera blephariglottis*) appearing later in the season in the same habitat. The plant seems to be fairly common in an area one year, then rather uncommon the next. This species is found from Newfoundland to Minnesota; in the mountains it ranges as far south as the Carolinas. It is rare in our area but has been recorded in both counties as far north as the central Bruce Peninsula. It is somewhat more frequent in Grey County south of the Bruce Peninsula. After flowering, the small leaf which had clasped the purplish stem during blooming emerges and grows to a length of about 8 centimetres as the fruit is ripening.

Description
Height 8-18 cm.
Leaf solitary, lanceolate, 5-12 cm x 2-8 mm, arising from the upper
   bract on the scape.
Scape arising from a bulbous corm with 1-3 blunt bracts at base.
Floral bract, scale-like, triangular, 3 x 2 mm.
Flower solitary, showy, rose-magenta to rose-white, terminating stem.
Sepals oblanceolate, lateral sepals falcate, oblique, 2-4 cm x 6-9 mm.
Lateral petals linear-oblique, curved, 2-3 cm x 5-8 mm.
Lip 2-3 x 1-2 cm, indistinctly 3-lobed, obovate. Lateral lobes short,
   broadly triangular. Mid-lobe curved downward, expanded,
   margins crenulate, erose, marked or veined with deep purple.
   Centre with yellow crests toward base, becoming fleshy and
   fringed toward apex. No spur.
Column 2-3.5 cm x 7-10 mm, elongated. Flattened with lateral wings.
   Erose at apex, pink. Anther on the front below apex with
   2 pairs of soft yellow-green pollinia.
Flowers: June to early July.

Capsule ellipsoid, erect, 2.5 x 1.5 cm.

Genus:
Calopogon R. Brown
Grass Pink, Calopogon

The Latin name is made up of the Greek words *pogon* (as with Pogonia) and *callos* (beauty) giving "beautiful beard." The name "Grass Pink" refers to the pink flowers and the grass-like leaves. There are four species of Calopogon, with only one species ranging far enough north to occur in this area. Members of this genus are different from other orchids in that the ovary does not twist so that the lip is in the uppermost position on the flower. What appears in the "usual" position of the lip is a large colourful column.

4. Grass Pink
Calopogon tuberosus (**L.**) **BSP.** [*Calopogon pulchellus*]
Grass Pink, Calopogon

Botanists have named this plant *tuberosus* (Latin) in reference to the solid corms that allow the species to survive hard years and reproduce vegetatively in good years. The ability to survive and reproduce has made this orchid familiar to many North American naturalists, who find the name Grass Pink apt because of the delicate colour of the flowers and the decidedly grassy basal leaf.

Since the lip is located uppermost in the flower, the Grass Pink has a special and amusing method of pollination. To be successful, the pollinating insect must be relatively heavy as the lip functions somewhat like a spring-loaded hinge. When the blossom opens, the lip holds its delicate beard of yellow stamen-like hairs stiffly upwards, soon attracting Bumble Bees. As the bees land on the "imitation stamens," the hinge at the base of the lip drops them on to the large, curving column that projects out below. The impact causes some pollen to be detached. The bee carries the pollen off to another flower and the process is repeated. To the human eye, the antics of flower and insect provide entertainment in addition to the pleasure of the magenta and gold beauty of these blossoms.

Grass Pink can be found normally in unshaded sites such as fens, soggy marl flats or less commonly here, in lush mats of *Sphagnum* moss. It is accompanied by such plants as Rose Pogonia (*Pogonia ophioglossoides*), Pitcher Plant (*Sarracenia purpurea*) and Bog Sedges (*Carex spp*). This plant is slightly more common and widespread in this area than Rose Pogonia, but is still rather uncommon overall. It tolerates a variety of habitats throughout its extensive range in eastern North America, as far south as Cuba. These plants can suffer from much "picking pressure," as the blooms may grow "by the handfuls." Flowers can be found from mid-June through most of July, occasionally into early August.

Description
Height 10-42 cm.
Leaves basal, 1-2, linear and grass-like, up to 30 x ±2 cm.
Raceme lax, flowers 3-8, rarely 12. Floral bracts ovate-acuminate, 6 x 3 mm.
Flowers large, pink to rose-purple or magenta-crimson, rarely white,
    opening successively a few at a time, not resupinate.
Dorsal sepal narrowly oblong, acute, 2-2.5 cm x 5-10 mm.
Lateral sepals ovate, oblique, apiculate, 1.5-2.5 x 1.0-1.3 cm.
Lateral petals with a short claw, ovate-lanceolate or oblong elliptic,
    often slightly constricted, ±2 cm x 4-10 mm.
Lip uppermost, 1-2 cm x 6-8 mm, with 2 ill-defined lateral lobes and a
    prominent broadly dilated or triangular middle lobe. Central
    portion of lip densely bearded with short, cream hairs with
    orange knobs.
Column 1-2 cm x 6-9 mm. Prominent, strongly curved, winged on each
    side. No spur.
Flowers: Mid-June to August.
Capsule ellipsoid, 3-angled, prominently 6-ribbed, 1-2 cm x 3-8 mm.

Genus:
Calypso Salisbury

Salisbury, the English botanist who named this genus in 1805 when it was introduced from Canada, was so impressed by its beauty that he called it after Calypso, the legendary sea nymph of Greek mythology who hid Odysseus on her secluded island and, with her enchantments, detained him for seven years. There is only one species with a circumpolar distribution. However, it can be divided into four, geographically separated, varieties which occur in Northern Europe and Asia, Japan, the Pacific Northwest and in boreal regions of North America.

5. Calypso
Calypso bulbosa (L.) Oakes
Calypso, Fairy Slipper

The species name *bulbosa* is a Latin adjective meaning "with a bulb" and refers to the corm produced annually at the base of this plant. All agree on the beauty of this Fairy Slipper. D. S. Correll (1950) spoke for many when he stated that, " Few if any of our native orchids possess the sheer beauty and loveliness of the Fairy Slipper. The first time I came upon this little orchid . . . I looked at the flowers with the feeling that at last I was indeed looking upon the most beautiful terrestrial orchid in North America." In this area, it is almost entirely restricted to the Bruce Peninsula, mainly the northern part. Calypso is mostly difficult to find despite its brightly coloured flower. This bloom of mauve, white, reddish-brown and golden yellow seldom rises above the tops of one's shoes. Calypso is our earliest orchid, with its peak of flowering being from mid-May to June. Calypso can be found in the company of plants such as early Violets (*Viola* spp.), Twinflower (*Linnaea borealis*), Lesser Rattlesnake Plantain (*Goodyera repens*) and Striped Coralroot (*Corallorhiza striata*), all of which share the shaded knolls and thickets of spruce, fir and cedar woods that are this delicate plant's refuge.

The Calypso shuns heat and throughout the summer all living traces of the plant disappear. Only in the early fall does a single, pleated, dark green heart-shaped leaf reappear amongst the thin leaf litter of the woodland floor. This leaf appears earlier in the fall than that of Putty Root (*Aplectrum hyemale*) and disappears later. The leaf persists under winter snows until the spring blooming period, thus building up a store of nutrients in the corm. Once a flowering colony is found, it is often possible to count many of these leaves that do not have a bloom in that particular year. Calypso is most common in the west; its rarity in eastern North America may be somewhat due to its reluctance to set seed here. Capsules are rarely seen.

Description
Height ±10 cm. Stem smooth.
Leaf solitary, basal, cordate-ovate to elliptic, apex rounded to acute,
  3-6 x 2-5 cm, dark to bluish green, appears in autumn,
  over-winters.
Scape with 2-3 transparent sheaths. Bract lanceolate, 7-15 mm long.
Flower solitary.
Sepals and lateral petals spreading, 1-2 cm x 3-5 mm, pinkish-purple,
  rarely whitish.
Lip ± 2 x 1 cm, saccate, white with yellowish 2-pronged apex, streaked
  with reddish-brown inside.
Apron formed from edges of lip, covers lower part of sac, white with
  pinkish-purple edges and spots, crested with three rows of
  golden hairs.
Column petal-like, overhanging lip, 8-12 mm long, pinkish-purple. No spur.
Flowers: early May to June (to the beginning of July in the far north of the area).
Fruit a capsule, erect, ellipsoid-cylindric, 2-3 cm long.

Genus:
Coeloglossum Hartman

This genus has been named from the Greek words *koilos* and *glossa* which together mean "hollow tongue," referring to minute features of the lip that lead to the tiny, pea-shaped spur. These distinguish the single species of this genus from other members of the former *Habenaria* group.

6. Long Bracted Green Orchid
Coeloglossum viride (L.) Hartman var. *virescens* (Muhl.) Luer
[*Habenaria viridis*, *H. bracteata*]
Long Bracted Green Orchid, Frog Orchid

This is the "greenest of green orchids"; both the species and variety names are derived from *viridis* the Latin word for green. Indeed, the only other colour on the plant is an occasional faint rose in the centre of the unassuming flowers. This orchid seems to be designed to be inconspicuous; the plant looks like a spire of leaves with little flowers hidden at the base of the leafy bracts. The flowers have a rounded "cap" with the lip projecting straight down below this.

The species as a whole is circumboreal. The European variety is known affectionately in England as the "Frog Orchid." The Long Bracted Green Orchid is definitely a plant of rich woods, growing in both deciduous, temperate and, further north, boreal forests. In this area, it is mainly restricted to upland deciduous forests on various soils, including rich loam over dolostone bedrock, even though it requires acid or subacid soil.

A pleasant stroll through a rich sugar maple forest in late spring or early summer might reveal the Green Orchid alone or in small groups amongst plants such as Squirrel Corn (*Dicentra canadensis*), *Hepatica* sp. and White Trillium (*Trillium grandiflorum*). It is more prevalent in Grey than in Bruce County and is very rare on the upper Bruce Peninsula.

Description
Height 10-40 cm.
Stem leafy, all leaves clasping the stem. Lower leaves obovate to oblanceolate. Upper leaf blades reduced, lanceolate, obtuse or acute. Largest leaves 5-15 x 2-8 cm.
Spike 6-20 cm long with 5 to 35 flowers, dense or lax.
Lowermost floral bracts 3-5 times larger than flowers, linear, acuminate and conspicuous. Upper bracts much reduced. Flowers green.
Petals and sepals somewhat connivent and forming a hood over the pendant lip.
Dorsal sepal ovate, 3-6 x ±3 mm.
Lateral sepals ovate, oblique, 4-6 x 2-3 mm.
Lateral petals linear, 3-5 mm long.
Lip prominent, narrow oblong, apex 2-3 toothed (middle tooth usually smaller or obscure), 5-10 x 2-4 mm near apex, occasionally tinged with rose or red-brown. Spur very short, sac-like.
Column short.
Flowers: mid-May (rarely early May) through June, rarely later.
Capsules ellipsoid, 7-10 mm long, often with the flowers remaining in good condition as it ripens.

Genus: *Corallorhiza* Ruppius ex Gagnebin
Coralroots

One scarcely needs to translate the botanical name of this genus, especially in light of the English name. It is derived from the Greek words *korallion* and *rhiza*, meaning "coral root" and refers to the remarkable root system of these plants which is fragile, multi-branched, and coralloid. All twelve species in this genus are saprophytic or root parasites. None rely completely on photosynthesis. All are found in Central or North America, with only one, *Corallorhiza trifida*, being circumboreal. Four species are found in this area. In all of them, the column is rather broad and slightly incurved with a terminal anther. It is shorter than the perianth and joined to the lateral sepals at its base, sometimes forming a small rotund spur.

7. Spotted Coralroot

Corallorhiza maculata (**Rafinesque**) **Rafinesque**
Spotted Coralroot

The Latin word *maculatus* means "spotted" and refers to the stain-like madder spots that often decorate its otherwise plain flower parts and sparkling white lip. However, these dots are neither consistent nor unique to this species. In fact, all colours of the flowering spike are quite variable and this has resulted in the naming of several forms. The following five have been reported from the Bruce-Grey area:
1) forma *flavida* (Peck) Cockerell – With an orange-yellow stem and sheaths, lemon-yellow flowers with an unspotted white lip.
2) forma *intermedia* Farwell – A predominantly brown plant with the stem and fruits light greyish brown and the sheaths dark purplish-brown.
3) forma *punicea* H. H. Bartlet – A plant without a trace of brown, but with the stem and fruit lavender or purple and the sheaths much paler than the stem.
4) forma *maculata* with a pinkish-purple stem.
5) an unnamed purple form which flowers earlier than the other forms.

The Spotted Coralroot is one of the most complex orchid species in this area and provides much intriguing variation which is made accessible by its relative frequency. The exception is forma *flavida* which is very rare and only known to exist from the central part of the Bruce Peninsula northwards. Spotted Coralroot can be found across the continent from Newfoundland to southern British Columbia in boreal and northern temperate woods and even occurs as far south as the mountains of Mexico and Guatemala. It is the most frequent of the saprophytic orchids growing in the Georgian Bay area, drawing its nutrients from decaying vegetable matter on the soil surface. It is found in rich, dryish, mixed coniferous and broad leaved deciduous woods and forests, including pine plantations. The stalk of this plant appears above ground level only while flowering and producing seeds. Open flowers may be found at any time between the second week of June to August.

Description
Height 12-50 cm. Stem stout or slender, smooth, leafless, madder-purple, brownish or yellowish with several tubular sheaths on the lower part.
Raceme lax, 2-30 flowers. Bracts minute, subulate, translucent, 1.5-3 mm long.
Flowers similar in colour to the upper part of the stem but a darker shade.
Sepals and lateral petals linear to oblong-lanceolate, obtuse to acute, 6-8 x 1-2 mm, spotted or unspotted.
Lip oblong-quadrate to obovate with 2 small lateral lobes. Terminal lobe broadly rounded, deflexed. 2 parallel ridges in centre.
White usually spotted magenta-crimson or madder. No spur.
Flowers: second week of June to August.
Capsules drooping, ovoid or ellipsoid, 1-2.5 cm long, diameter 6 mm.

8. Autumn Coralroot
Corallorhiza odontorhiza **(Willd.) Nutt.**
Autumn Coralroot, Late Coralroot

The Latin name is derived from the Greek words *odonto* meaning "tooth" and *rhiza* meaning "root" and refers to the tooth-like appearance of the swollen base of the stem.

Autumn Coralroot is a provincially rare Carolinian species, found in one pine plantation on the Bruce Peninsula. There is a possibility that it was introduced with pine seedlings from the provincial tree nursery at St. Williams in Norfolk County, where it was once locally common. The dull purplish colour and comparatively small size combined with its late flowering time, when leaves are beginning to fall, make this species difficult to spot. Although most Ontario plants have essentially closed flowers, we have the showier, open-flowered form. It finishes blooming later than all the other orchids in this area. Its peak blooming season is, on average, late September but, in some years, it does not appear at all. Our area is very much on the northern edge of its range which extends as far south as Mexico.

Description
Height 6-16 cm. Base of stem swollen, purplish to brownish, few
    sheathing scales.
Raceme lax, 5-15 small flowers.
Sepals and lateral petals lanceolate, 3-4 mm long, yellowish to greenish
    to purplish, projecting out over the column.
Lip obovate, broad and deflexed at free end, 3-4 mm long. Whitish,
    purple spotted.
Spur small at the top of the ovary.
Flowers: August to October or early November.
Capsule ovoid, drooping, 5 x 4 mm.

9. Striped Coralroot
Corallorhiza striata Lindley
Striped Coralroot

The Latin *striatus* means "striate" or "striped." Striped Coralroot is one of our most striking plants. The distinctive red striping of the flower is the feature by which it may be identified immediately. The flowers are dime-sized and ". . . boldly striped and edged in crimson on a background of yellow to pink, and they glow as if electrified when struck by rays of sunlight from behind" (Luer, 1975). The translucent sparkle of these flowers excites comparisons with jewellery, and the intensity of red-purple colouring makes this by far our most attractive Coralroot.

Flowering in late May, this is the first Coralroot to bloom. On the Bruce Peninsula this puts it in good company with the delicate Calypso or Fairy Slipper (*Calypso bulbosa*). Although these two plants may share the same habitat, the Striped Coralroot is tolerant of drier and more open woods. As it also flowers on until the beginning of July, there is a very good chance of discovering some plants early on in an orchid spotting career. In this area, the Striped Coralroot occurs in coniferous (particularly cedar) to deciduous woods in which it tends to prefer drier sites. It has also been found in pine plantations, and sometimes along roadsides.

The Striped Coralroot rarely grows more than 35-40 cm high here. Like the other Coralroots, it sometimes forms dense clumps. Along with the Alaska Orchid (*Piperia unalascensis*) and Menzies' Rattlesnake Plantain (*Goodyera oblongifolia*), this species presents a challenge in plant geography and history. These plants, common in the western mountains, become rarer eastward, with the Bruce Peninsula being one of the eastern centres of local abundance. This fact was earlier thought to be evidence for an ice-free area in the vicinity of the Bruce Peninsula, but the occurrence here, of these orchids and other western plants, is more likely due to the land bridge westward through Manitoulin Island, which occurred at the time of the post-glacial pine maximum about 8,000 years ago.

Description
Height 10-40 cm. Stem leafless, madder purple to brownish-purple with
    3-4 slightly inflated sheaths at the base paler than the stem.
Raceme lax with 3-30 flowers. Floral bracts triangular, ±2 mm long.
Flowers pinkish-yellow or white, tinged and conspicuously striped with
    reddish purple, large for genus.
Sepals elliptic-oblong to obovate-elliptic, rounded at apex, 6-15 x 2.5-5 mm.
Lateral petals similar, slightly smaller.
Lip 6-12 x 6-8 mm, pendant, somewhat reflexed, fleshy, not lobed,
    suborbicular-elliptic to obovate-elliptic, concave, thickened
        margin involute, 3 stripes at base merging at apex. Bilobed
        callus near middle of base. No spur.
Flowers: late May to early July.
Capsules drooping, ellipsoid, 1-2 x ±1 cm.

10. Early Coralroot
Corallorhiza trifida **Chatelain**
Early Coralroot, Northern Coralroot

The botanical name for this species is derived from the Latin "trifidus" meaning "cleft into three parts" and refers to the three-lobed lip. This feature is shared with the Spotted Coralroot (*Corallorhiza maculata*), along with the white colour of the lip which frequently has purple spots. The English name, Northern Coralroot, is more distinctive as this species is circumboreal. Along with the Heart Leaved Twayblade (*Listera cordata*) and Blunt Leaf Rein Orchid (*Platanthera obtusata*), it circles the globe in the great belt of boreal forest. It is the only Coralroot found in Europe and Asia. This species responds well to "cold bottom" conditions.

Northern Coralroot is the only member of this genus with distinctly yellowish-green colouring in the stem and flowers. It is an early flowering plant and the best way to find the delicate flowers in their prime is to walk through cool, wet coniferous or mixed woods, pine plantations or, on the northern Bruce Peninsula, conifer-dominated uplands during the month of June. In well shaded areas, it can often be found growing in colonies of twenty or thirty plants near other small orchids such as Broad Leaved Twayblade (*Listera convallarioides*), Blunt Leaf Rein Orchid (*Platanthera obtusata*) or Lesser Rattlesnake Plantain (*Goodyera repens*). Later in the season, the Northern Coralroot remains recognizable because it develops distinctive fat yellowish drooping seed pods. These can be even more conspicuous than the flowers that preceded them. In this area, the plant occurs fairly frequently but not abundantly.

Description
Height 4-20 cm. Stem smooth, leafless, green or greenish-yellow with
  pale tubular sheaths at base.
Spike 3-20 flowered. Bracts minute, subulate, 1-2 mm long.
Flowers mostly pale greenish-yellow, sometimes tinged with
  red-brown.
Dorsal sepal oblanceolate, obtuse, ±6 x 1-2 mm.
Lateral sepals oblique, spreading, linear oblanceolate, ±6 x 1-2 mm
  above the middle.
Lateral petals oblanceolate, oblique, obtuse, ±5 x 1-2 mm, connivent
  with dorsal sepal forming hood over column.
Lip arcuate-recurved, 3-5 x 2-3 mm, 3-lobed with middle lobe
  expanded and rounded to truncate with undulate margins,
  lateral lobes like small triangular upturned teeth near the
  narrowed base, floor of lip with a pair of flattened ridges.
  No spur.
Flowers: late May to the beginning of July.
Capsules drooping at maturity, obovoid-ellipsoid, 8-12 mm long.

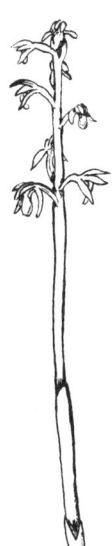

Genus:
Cypripedium L.
Lady's Slippers

There are approximately ten species of Lady's Slippers in the United States and Canada, but only one in Europe. Five species have been found in the Bruce-Grey area. The name of this genus is derived from Cypris, one of the names of Venus, the Greek goddess of love and beauty, and the Greek word *pedilon* meaning "shoe" in reference to the slipper-like lip which is the feature of this group. Hence the name Lady's Slipper for our most spectacular wild orchids. These are the orchids which attract the attention and admiration of all and this beauty often spells disaster. These orchids have been dug up, vandalized by photographers, picked in great bouquets, and generally abused by people who, in a vain attempt to capture and possess such loveliness, end by destroying it. In all species the column is declined over the opening of the lip with a fertile stamen on each side and a conspicuous staminode (sterile stamen) above which covers the tip of the style. Thus, insects attracted by the staminode and investigating the "slipper" pick up pollen from the fertile stamens.

11. Pink Moccasin Flower
Cypripedium acaule **Aiton**
Pink Moccasin Flower, Pink Lady's Slipper, Stemless Lady's Slipper

The Latin name "acaule" meaning "stemless" refers to the absence of any true aboveground stem. The flower has quite a long stalk or scape. This springs from a short underground stem from which the leaves also arise. The two or, rarely, three, dark green, strongly veined oval leaves clasp the bottom of the scape. They are silvery beneath and both they and the scape are covered with soft hairs. At least a hand's height above the handsome leaves hangs the showy flower. Here we see the reason for the names "slipper" and "moccasin," as the pink rose-veined lip of the flower is, indeed, slipper shaped to fit an elfin foot. The opening of the slipper is a narrow fissure, curved inward at the edges and running the length of the lip. This distinguishes the Moccasin Flower from other Lady's Slippers, whose openings are generally round. The other two petals are quite different from the lip, being long and narrow and lightly twisted. Their colour varies from yellow-green to purplish-brown. Along with the similarly coloured sepals they hang over protectively, framing the delicate "slipper."

The Stemless Lady's Slipper is found in acid conditions from Newfoundland to Alberta in boreal and temperate regions becoming rare in the west and extending as far south as Alabama, Georgia and South Carolina. In this region it grows mostly in acid conifer-dominated swamps or wooded bogs. It can also be found growing in dry sandy or rocky places if the soil requirements are right, particularly under Jack Pines in the northern part of the Bruce Peninsula. This species is less common on the Bruce Peninsula than farther south in Bruce and Grey Counties. Blossoms appear between the end of May and beginning of July. In some swamps it is possible to count dozens of "moccasins" without moving. The effect is of a green carpet spattered with pink paint. One cannot walk across for fear of crushing the living design.

Description
Height 15-40 cm.
Leaves 2 to 3, basal, sheathing the scape. Elliptical 8-24 x 3-12 cm.
Leaves silvery below, strongly veined and dark green above.
Leaves and scape hairy.
One lanceolate, green bract arching over flower. ±4 x ±1.5 cm.
Flower solitary (rarely two). Scape 12-40 cm long.
Sepals and lateral petals yellow-green to purplish-brown.
Dorsal sepal 4-5 cm x 5-17 mm, elliptic-lanceolate, arched.
Lateral sepals 3-4.5 x 1-2 cm, united behind the flower.
Lateral petals lanceolate, 4-6 x ±1.5 cm, spreading, somewhat twisted.
Lip forming a pouch, ±5 x ±3 cm, showy pink (rarely white) with red or purplish veining.
Opening an elongate fissure on upper surface. No spur.
Flowers: end of May to early July.
Capsule football-shaped, ribbed, dark brown ±3.5 cm long.

12. Ram's Head Lady's Slipper
Cypripedium arietinum R. Brown
Ram's Head Lady's Slipper

Both the English and Latin names (*arietinum* means "of a ram") refer to the fancied resemblance of the flower to the head of a charging ram. This is the smallest and most inconspicuous of the Lady's Slippers and for this reason it is a challenging one to find. Usually, it is found standing solitary or in loose groups, on dunes or in thin soil on bedrock. Locations are generally towards Lake Huron and, normally, thinly shaded so that the soil remains cool, such as under Jack or Red Pines. It is also known from one acid wooded swamp.

It is a small leafy plant growing to a maximum of 20 cm. The narrow leaves spiral around the stem. The tiny "slipper" is white, criss-crossed with dark red veins (on rare specimens these may be very faint). Unlike other Lady's Slippers, the lip is elongated into a downward pointing cone at the "toe" end. The top of the lip is covered with downy white hairs. The two long, narrow, greenish-brown lateral petals point down each side of the lip; behind lie the three sepals, the dorsal sepal on top, the lateral sepals behind the flower. Unlike our other four species of Lady's Slippers, the lateral sepals are not united as one ventral sepal under the "slipper."

Ram's Head Lady's Slipper is in flower from the last ten days of May until just past mid-June in this area. It is almost entirely restricted to the Bruce Peninsula, where it is found mostly between Highway 6 and the Lake Huron shoreline. It is probably more common on the Bruce Peninsula and Manitoulin Island than elsewhere in Ontario. This plant is rare through the rest of its range, which extends from Nova Scotia to Manitoba, south from Connecticut to Minnesota.

Description
Height 10-24 cm. Stem slender and somewhat hairy, 2-3 sheathing scales at base.
Leaves, 3-5, spiralling around stem above scales. Blue-green elliptical, 5-10 x 1-2.5 cm.
Flowers solitary. Scape 5-15 cm.
Lateral petals and sepals greenish-brown, linear, 1.5-2.5 cm long.
Lip 1.5-2.5 x 1-2 cm, prolonged downward into a small conical pouch. White, veined with dark red or madder.
Mouth of lip covered with white hairs. Opening circular. No spur.
Flowers: last 10 days of May until mid-June.
Capsule ±3 cm long, obliquely ellipsoid and sub-erect.

13. & 14. Yellow Lady's Slipper
Cypripedium parviflorum Salisbury
[*Cypripedium calceolus* L.]

There are two varieties of this species. They may be difficult to separate in the field.

13. Large Yellow Lady's Slipper
Cypripedium parviflorum Salisbury var. *pubescens* (Willd.) O.W. Knight
[*Cypripedium calceolus* L. var. *pubescens* (Willd.) Correll; *C. pubescens*]

The varietal name *pubescens* refers to the glandular hairiness of the stems and leaves. These hairs are quite toxic to some people, causing a very irritating rash.

From late May to the beginning of July, but mainly in the first half of June, the Yellow Lady's Slipper opens its beautiful blooms. it can be found growing in full sunlight and in shadow, typically in openings in evergreen forests or on dry open rocky areas. This is an ecologically versatile species, occurring in many types of woodlands, wet to dry, coniferous to deciduous, and on a variety of substrates. However, it tends to be somewhat of a calcicole, which explains its abundance on the Bruce Peninsula, where it may be more common than in any other part of Ontario. It has the habit of growing in compact clumps, sometimes containing over fifty stems. The plant is leafy and slender and can reach a height of 40 to 50 centimetres, although usually less. It is crowned with a regal bloom whose egg-shaped golden pouch is taut like an inflated balloon, and thrust forward. The mouth and inside of the pouch is streaked and spotted with deep madder-red, the brownish or greenish-red petals are long and narrow and somewhat spirally twisted, flaring out from each side of the yellow lip. Behind are the similarly coloured sepals, the dorsal one arched over the flower and the two lateral ones united behind, as though to further emphasize the flower's beauty. The great majority of our Yellow Lady's Slippers are essentially pure specimens of this variety. Unlike var. *makasin*, they are not distinctly scented. The Large Yellow Lady's Slipper occurs from the Yukon to Newfoundland, south to New Mexico in the west and 33ºN latitude in the southeastern States.

Description

Height 10-50 cm. Leaves and stem densely pubescent.
Leaves 3-6 (rarely 2), 2 ranked, somewhat sheathing the stem,
 elliptical, strongly ribbed, 5-12 cm x 3-8 cm.
Flower solitary (rarely 2), peduncle slender, subtended by a
 large, leafy bract. Scent is mostly lacking.
Sepals and petals greenish-yellowish-brownish to madder purple.
Dorsal sepal 3-8 x 1-3 cm, ovate-lanceolate, arched over flower.
Lateral sepals united, 2.5-8 x ±2.5 cm.
Petals linear-lanceolate, usually spirally twisted, 4-9 x ±1 cm.
Lip an inflated "slipper," 3-5 cm long, pale to deep yellow
 outside, spotted and streaked with brownish-purple
 inside. Opening oval.
Staminode triangular, yellow with red spots, 1 x 1 cm. No spur.
Flowers: late May to early July, mostly in the first half of June.
Capsule ellipsoid, nearly erect.

14. Small Yellow Lady's Slipper
Cypripedium parviflorum Salisbury var. *makasin* (Farwell) Sheviak
[*Cypripedium calceolus* L. var. *parviflorum* (Salisb.) Fernald; *C. parviflorum*]

This is the smaller variety of the Yellow Lady's Slipper. Appropriately enough, the Latin word "parviflorum" means "small flowered." The two forms of Yellow Lady's Slippers intergrade rather extensively in our area, so only those which are more or less pure specimens of the variety *makasin* are described here.

The floral difference between the two varieties is considerably greater than the vegetative difference. The flower is smaller, slightly more dainty and more closely resembles the rarer European plant than that of var. *pubescens*. The lip is compressed laterally in the Large Yellow Lady's Slippers, whereas it is compressed vertically in this variety. The lip is bright golden-yellow, and the petals and sepals are dark purplish-mahogany. The two long, narrow petals are tightly spiralled and glossy. The flower has a delicious fragrance, suggestive of vanilla. The small Yellow Lady's Slipper tends to grow in somewhat more acidic, swampy locations. Its range is from Newfoundland through the Maritimes, Quebec and Ontario to Minnesota and northwest as far as British Columbia and Alaska.

Description – only features that are different from var. pubescens are noted here.
Height 10-35 cm.
Oval leaves and stem less pubescent than var. *pubescens*.
Sepals and petals dark purplish-mahogany, glossy (darker than var. *pubescens*) up to 5 cm long.
Lip bright golden-yellow, 2-3 cm long, an inflated pouch compressed vertically.
Opening and inside of pouch spotted and streaked with purple.
Flowers fragrant, somewhat like vanilla.
Staminode similar shape to var. *pubescens*, deep yellow with purple spots, 8 x 8 mm.
Flowers: slightly later than var. *pubescens*, from the end of May to early July.

15. Small White Lady's Slipper
Cypripedium candidum **Muhl. ex Willd.**
Small White Lady's Slipper

The Latin word *candidus* means "shining white," a most appropriate description for this flower with its white egg-shaped slipper offset by the glowing golden staminode. This is the most sun-loving of all our Lady's Slippers. It is closely allied to the Yellow Lady's Slipper (*Cypripedium calceolus*). The marly soil of the fens of our area should provide suitable habitat for this smaller species of lady's slipper. However, there is only one record, from a location in the vicinity of Southampton and Port Elgin and not since 1925. Extensive development along the shore of Lake Huron since that time with the consequent changes in drainage patterns has resulted in the loss of other species associated with similar habitats in the same general area. In any case, it would have been on the northern edge of its range which extends from New York to North Dakota and south as far as Missouri.

The white "slipper" with violet veins inside and no suggestion of colour outside and the golden staminode together with the greenish, sometimes red-striped sepals and lateral petals would make this species easy to distinguish from all our other orchids. A real triumph awaits the discoverer of this elusive charmer!

Description
Height 10 to 25 cm.
Flower solitary – rarely 2.
Leaves 3-4, elliptic to lanceolate, 7-12 x 2-5 cm. A few
    sheathing scales below.
Dorsal sepal and lateral petals 3-4 cm long, greenish,
    often red-striped, lanceolate. Petals slightly longer
    and twisted. Lateral sepals joined almost to the apices.
Lip waxy-white, ±2 cm long, veined with violet inside.
Staminode ovate, yellow with purple spots. No spur.
Flowers: May to June.
Capsule ellipsoid, erect, 3 cm long.

16. Showy (Queen) Lady's Slipper
Cypripedium reginae **Walter**
Showy Lady's Slipper, Queen Lady's Slipper

The specific name *reginae* meaning "queen" pays homage to this beautiful plant. As the largest and showiest in Canada, it is indeed the queen of our orchids. This robust plant with its leafy stem is crowned by showy pink and white blossoms which catch the eye and cannot be mistaken for any other flower. The "slipper" is white, normally suffused with pale to deep rose pink. Sometimes the slipper is so heavily streaked that it appears to be pink or rose. Both the petals and sepals are waxy-white. Two narrow white petals spread out like wings above the lip, while the dorsal sepal arches over it and the two lateral sepals are joined into one behind the flower. Over the round entrance to the slipper arches the prominent staminode, or sterile stamen, which is triangular and white with yellow tipping or spotting. Along with the flower's delicate fragrance, this adds the finishing touch of elegance to the whole ensemble. Occasionally, a completely white form will be found. In this case, the larger size will distinguish it from the Small White Lady's Slipper (*Cypripedium candidum*).

Like the Yellow Lady's Slipper, the hairs are irritating and toxic, causing an itchy rash on some people. For this reason alone, it is best not to handle the plant. Grazing animals are discouraged by the fact that the floral tissues contain needle-sharp crystals, preventing animals such as deer from developing a taste for such exotic food.

In our area, this flower appears a little later than the other Lady's Slippers – normally, from the middle of June to the middle of July. It can be found in swampy or boggy woods, and in openings in cedar swamps where plants such as Marsh Fern (*Thelypteris palustris*) and sedges (*Carex* spp.) grow. Occasionally it is to be seen in wet, open roadside ditches. Showy Lady's Slipper is a calcicole which responds well to "cold bottom" conditions and is more abundant in this area than in most other parts of the province. It is found throughout Bruce and Grey Counties but is most common on the Bruce Peninsula. It ranges from Newfoundland to Minnesota, south to Georgia and Missouri.

Description
Height 20-80 cm.
Leaves 3-6, 10-25 x 6-16 cm, spirally sheathing stem,
    bright green ovate-lanceolate, strongly ribbed and folded, pubescent.
Flowers 1 or 2 (3) subtended by a leafy bract.
Sepals and petals waxy-white.
Dorsal sepal ovate-orbicular, 3-4.5 x 2.5-3.5 cm. Lateral sepals united.
Petals ovate-lanceolate, 2.5-4 x 1-1.5 cm.
Lip an inflated pouch, 2.5-5 cm long, white with red or rosy pink veins which are grooved in white.
    Rarely pure white. Opening oval. Fragrant.
Staminode prominent, cordate-ovate, white, yellow tipped or spotted. No spur.
Flowers: mid-June (rarely early June) to late July.
Capsule ellipsoid, 3-4.5 x 1.5 cm.

Genus:
Epipactis Zinn
Helleborine

The English name for this genus comes from the Latin word *helleborus* referring to the supposed similarity of these plants to the hellebores, a group of poisonous plants in the **Ranunculaceae** (Buttercup) family, hence the name helleborine. The genus has about twenty species in Europe and Asia but only two in North America. *Epipactis helleborine* was introduced in eastern North America, the other is native to the western mountains. The introduced species has now spread as far west as Vancouver Island.

17. Helleborine
Epipactis helleborine (L.) Crantz
Helleborine

Helleborine is one of our most common orchids. It is the only representative of the genus in our area but it is found throughout the region. It grows in many different types of habitat such as gravelly roadsides, old trails through forests, sheltered sandy beaches, dense conifer forests or even in lawns. It is especially common in pine plantations. The veiny, dark green leaves are sessile and become smaller near the top of the stalk. They are smooth on the underside and somewhat hairy above. The general aspect of the plant is sufficiently like that of a Lady's Slipper to catch your attention. The resemblance ends when it is seen that the flowers are smaller and in a long, tapering, somewhat one-sided raceme which is tipped over at the top when in bud. The general effect of the plant is rather coarse and unattractive but a closer study of the small flowers is worthwhile. The petals are pale green to pink with the lip greenish, tinged with purple or rose-red. Each flower is on a short stem which arises from an elongated leafy bract at the end. Characteristic of this plant, is the purplish coloration of the stem from ground level up to the point of attachment of the lowest leaf. The way the plant arches over when young is also a very good mark.

Late July through August is the time to look for this orchid in bloom, though its prominent leaves give it away before that. Its spike of nodding brown seed pods is easily recognized later in the fall. Very rarely, it may bloom well into October. At a time when many other orchids have finished blooming, it is interesting to come upon this tolerant species along the trails and roadsides of this area. In a family famous for the rarity and beauty of its members, of plants which typically have to be sought out in obscure places, it is strange to find one like Helleborine which positively thrusts itself upon your attention and is, moreover, strange rather than beautiful.

Description
Height variable from 15 to 65 cm. Stem slender to sturdy.
Leaves variable, 3-10, more or less clasping the stem, largest leaves
      near the middle of the stem.
Elliptic or narrowly lanceolate, plicate and veiny, 3-18 x 1.5-8.5 cm.
Raceme, up to 30 cm long, one sided, tapering, flowers few to numerous.
 Leafy bracts elliptic to linear-lanceolate, the lower ones longer
      than the flowers, up to 5 cm long and 1.8 cm wide.
Flowers whitish-green, often streaked with purple and rose-red,
      ±2 cm long.
Sepals ovate-lanceolate, concave, ±12 x ±5 mm. Petals slightly smaller,
      ovate-elliptic.
Lip about 10-15 x 4-8 mm, constricted near middle, lower part fleshy,
      tip with a raised fleshy callus.
Column short and wide with one sessile anther. No spur.
Flowers: late July to August, very rarely until October.
Capsules drooping, oblong, ±1 cm long.

Genus:
Galearis Rafinesque

The Latin name is from *galea* meaning "helmet" and refers to the hood over the column, which is created by the connivent petals and sepals. This genus was created to accommodate one North American species, which had features that prevented it from being included in the *Orchis* genus. It now includes a second species, *Galearis cyclochila,* found in eastern Asia.

These two species have a very short rhizome with several fibrous to fleshy roots which lack tubers. There is a pair of basal leaves between which a scape-like stem emerges. The large leaf-like floral bracts surpass the flowers which are in a loose raceme. The lip is entire and extends into a spur.

18. Showy Orchis

Galearis spectabilis **(L.) Raf.** [*Orchis spectabilis*]
Showy Orchis

The name is from the Latin *spectabilis* which means "notable" or "remarkable" and refers to the showy flowers produced by this plant. It can be found in rich deciduous forests, growing in thick layers of decaying humus This is one of the earliest flowering orchids in this area, typically coming into flower from mid to late May, before the trees are fully leafed out. It usually grows alone or in small clusters. The Showy Orchis can be found in the company of such species as Trilliums (*Trillium* spp.), Jack-in-the-Pulpit (*Arisaema triphyllum*), and Canada Violet (*Viola canadensis*).

The leaves spread on either side of the flower stem. The pink or mauve flower parts contrast well with the snowy white lip. Very rarely, the flower is entirely white, faint pink, or rich red-lilac. The Showy Orchis is more prevalent in Grey than in Bruce County, where it occurs, infrequently, north to the central Bruce Peninsula.
Its range is from New Brunswick to Minnesota, south to Arkansas and Georgia.

Description
Height 8-20 cm. Plant smooth and succulent.
Leaves 2, basal, subopposite, suborbicular to broadly elliptic, fleshy, dark green, up to ±14 x ±8 cm, bases folded into distinct peduncles sheathing the stem and subtended by 2 scarious sheaths.
Occasional floral bract, leaf-like, lanceolate, 2-7 x 1-1.5 cm.
Up to 15 flowers in a loose, terminal raceme.
Sepals purplish, elliptic-lanceolate, 12-20 x 6-7 mm, lateral sepals oblique.
Lateral petals purplish, linear, 12-18 x 3 mm, connivent with sepals over column.
Lip white, ovate, entire, obtuse, with a wavy margin, 10-20 x 7-16 mm.
Column stout, 7 x 4 mm. Spur stout, slightly clavate, 10-20 x 3 mm.
Flowers: mid-May to June.
Capsule erect, ellipsoid, 2 x 1 cm.

1. Small Round Leaved Orchis
Amerorchis rotundifolia

2. Putty Root Orchid
Aplectrum hyemale

3. Arethusa Orchid
Arethusa bulbosa

4. Grass Pink Orchid
Calopogon tuberosus

5. Calypso, Fairy Slipper
Calypso bulbosa

6. Long Bracted Green Orchid
Coeloglossum viride

7. Spotted Coralroot
Corallorhiza maculata

8. Autumn Coralroot
Corallorhiza odontorhiza

9. Striped Coralroot
Corallorhiza striata

10. Early Coralroot
Corallorhiza trifida

11. Pink Lady's Slipper (Moccasin Flower)
Cypripedium acaule

12. Ram's Head Lady's Slipper
Cypripedium arietinum

13. Large Yellow Lady's Slipper
Cypripedium parviflorum var. *pubescens*

14. Small Yellow Lady's Slipper
Cypripedium parviflorum var. *makasin*

15. Small White Lady's Slipper
Cypripedium candidum

16. Showy (Queen) Lady's Slipper
Cypripedium reginae

17. Helleborine
Epipactis helleborine

18. Showy Orchis
Galearis spectabilis

19. Menzies' Rattlesnake Plantain
Goodyera oblongifolia

20. Downy Rattlesnake Plantain
Goodyera pubescens

21. Dwarf Rattlesnake Plantain
Goodyera repens var. *ophioides*

22. Checkered Rattlesnake Plantain
Goodyera tesselata

23. Loesel's Twayblade
Liparis loeselii

24. Broad Lipped Twayblade
Listera convallarioides

25. Heart Leaved Twayblade
Listera cordata

26. European Common Twayblade
Listera ovata

27. White Adder's Mouth
Malaxis monophylla

28. Green Adder's Mouth
Malaxis unifolia

29. Alaska Orchid
Piperia unalascensis

30. White Fringed Orchis
Platanthera blephariglottis

31. Club Spur Orchid
Platanthera clavellata

32. Tall White Bog Orchid
Platanthera dilatata

33. Tubercled Orchid
Platanthera flava

34. Hooker's Orchid
Platanthera hookeri

35. Tall Northern Green Orchid
Platanthera aquilonis

36. Ragged Fringed Orchid
Platanthera lacera

37. Prairie Fringed Orchid
Platanthera leucophaea

38. Blunt Leaf Rein Orchid
Platanthera obtusata

39. Round Leaf Orchid
Platanthera orbiculata var. *orbiculata*

40. Large Round Leaved Orchid
Platanthera macrophylla

41. Small Purple Fringed Orchid
Platanthera psycodes

42. Rose Pogonia
Pogonia ophioglossoides

43. Case's Ladies' Tresses
Spiranthes casei

44. Nodding Ladies' Tresses
Spiranthes cernua

45. Slender Ladies' Tresses
Spiranthes lacera

46. Shining Ladies' Tresses
Spiranthes lucida

47. Great Plains Ladies' Tresses
Spiranthes magnicamporum

48. Hooded Ladies' Tresses
Spiranthes romanzoffiana

TABLE A:
CLIMATIC ZONES OF BRUCE AND GREY COUNTIES

	Bruce Peninsula		Lake Huron	Huron Slopes	Georgian Bay		Dundalk Upland
	Tobermory	Wiarton	Kincardine	Walkerton	Owen Sound	Meaford	Durham
Altitude (metres)	175	175	175	305	175	175	395
Mean Temp (°C)	6.1	6.1	7.2	6.7	6.7	6.7	5.6
Daily Temp Range (°C) – January	6.7	7.8	6.4	7.8	8.0	8.3	8.3
Daily Temp Range (°C) – July	10.0	10.6	11.1	12.8	12.2	11.1	13.4
Mean Frost Free Period (Days)	145	145	150	135	135	140	115
Length of Growing Season	195	195	205	200	195	190	185
Mean Annual Precipitation (cm)	81	86	86	92	91	81	102
Mean Annual Snowfall (cm)	220	285	254	285	285	265	285
Mean May-Sept. Precipitation (cm)	34	34	34	38	36	33	41

Adapted from Brown et al., 1980.

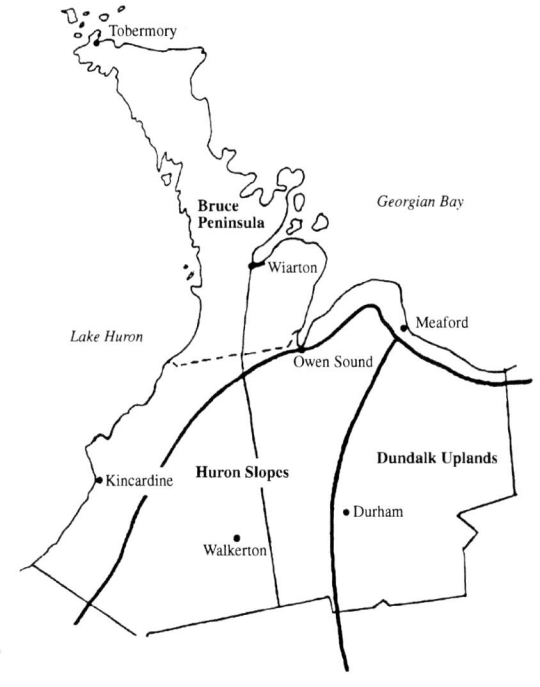

TABLE B:
CHART OF APPROXIMATE FLOWERING TIMES FOR THE ORCHIDS OF BRUCE AND GREY COUNTIES

NO.	SCIENTIFIC NAME	COMMON NAME	MAY	JUNE	JULY	AUG	SEPT
5	*Calypso bulbosa*	Calypso, Fairy Slipper					
6	*Coeloglossum viride*	Long Bracted Green Orchid					
18	*Galearis spectabilis*	Showy Orchis					
13	*Cypripedium parviflorum* var. *pubescens*	Large Yellow Lady's Slipper					
25	*Listera cordata*	Heart Leaved Twayblade					
9	*Corallorhiza striata*	Striped Coralroot					
12	*Cypripedium arietinum*	Ram's Head Lady's Slipper					
10	*Corallorhiza trifida*	Early Coralroot					
34	*Platanthera hookeri*	Hooker's Orchid					
15	*Cypripedium candidum*	Small White Lady's Slipper					
14	*Cypripedium parviflorum* var. *makasin*	Small Yellow Lady's Slipper					
11	*Cypripedium acaule*	Pink Lady's Slipper (Moccasin Flower)					
2	*Aplectrum hyemale*	Putty Root Orchid					
3	*Arethusa bulbosa*	Arethusa Orchid					
35	*Platanthera aquilonis*	Tall Northern Green Orchid					
26	*Listera ovata*	European Common Twayblade					
16	*Cypripedium reginae*	Showy (Queen) Lady's Slipper					
29	*Piperia unalascensis*	Alaska Orchid					
32	*Platanthera dilatata*	Tall White Bog Orchid					
1	*Amerorchis rotundifolla*	Small Round Leaved Orchis					
4	*Calopogon tuberosus*	Grass Pink Orchid					
46	*Spiranthes lucida*	Shining Ladies' Tresses					
38	*Platanthera obtusata*	Blunt Leaf Rein Orchid					
7	*Corallorhiza maculata*	Spotted Coralroot					

NO.	SCIENTIFIC NAME	COMMON NAME	JUNE	JULY	AUG	SEPT	OCT
23	*Liparis loeselii*	Loesel's Twayblade	••▬••				
33	*Platanthera flava*	Tubercled Orchid	•••▬••				
40	*Platanthera macrophylla*	Large Round Leaved Orchid	•••▬	••••			
42	*Pogonia ophioglossoides*	Rose Pogonia	•••▬	••••••••			
24	*Listera convallarioides*	Broad Lipped Twayblade	••▬•				
27	*Malaxis monophylla*	White Adder's Mouth	•••▬	••			
39	*Platanthera orbiculata*	Round Leaf Orchid	••••▬	▬•••			
36	*Platanthera lacera*	Ragged Fringed Orchid	••• ▬	••••			
28	*Malaxis unifolia*	Green Adder's Mouth	••• ▬	••••			
41	*Platanthera psycodes*	Small Purple Fringed Orchid	••▬	••••			
30	*Platanthera blephariglottis*	White Fringed Orchis		••• ▬ •••			
37	*Platanthera leucophaea*	Prairie Fringed Orchid		•••▬•••			
22	*Goodyera tesselata*	Checkered Rattlesnake Plantain		•••• ▬ ••••			
45	*Spiranthes lacera*	Slender Ladies' Tresses		••••▬	•••••••••	••	
7	*Epipactis helleborine*	Helleborine		•••▬	•••••••••	••••••••	
31	*Platanthera clavellata*	Club Spur Orchid		••• ▬ ••••			
48	*Spiranthes romanzoffiana*	Hooded Ladies' Tresses		•••▬	•••••••••	••	
20	*Goodyera pubescens*	Downy Rattlesnake Plantain		•••••• ▬	••••		
19	*Goodyera oblongifolia*	Menzies' Rattlesnake Plantain		••▬	•••••••	••	
21	*Goodyera repens* var. *ophioides*	Dwarf Rattlesnake Plantain		••▬	••		
44	*Spiranthes cernua*	Nodding Ladies' Tresses			•••• ▬	•••••	
8	*Corallorhiza odontorhiza*	Autumn Coralroot			•••••••▬	▬▬	••••
43	*Spiranthes casei*	Case's Ladies' Tresses			•▬••		
47	*Spiranthes magnicamporum*	Great Plains Ladies' Tresses				••▬	••

Note: Dots indicate first and last known flowering dates; solid lines indicate best flowering periods. Exceptional weather conditions may accelerate or retard flowering beyond normal limits.

TABLE C:
NATIONALLY AND PROVINCIALLY RARE ORCHIDS OF BRUCE AND GREY COUNTIES

Species		Argus		NHIC		COSEWIC & MNR
		Can	Ont	G	S	
Aplectrum hyemale	– Puttyroot	X	X	5	2	
Corallorhiza odontorhiza	– Autumn Coralroot	X	X	5	2	
Cypripedium arietinum	– Ram's Head Lady's Slipper			3	3	
Cypripedium candidum	– Small White Lady's Slipper	X	X	4	1	Endangered
Platanthera flava	– Tubercled Orchid			4	4	
Platanthera leucophaea	– Prairie Fringed Orchid	X	X	2	2	Endangered
Platanthera macrophylla	– Large Round Leaved Orchid		X	4	2	
Spiranthes magnicamporum	– Great Plains Ladies' Tresses	X	X	4	3	

Small White Lady's Slipper (*Cypripedium candidum*) is a historical record for Bruce County. It has not been reported from this area for over seventy years.

The "Argus" columns show the status of the species according to Argus *et al* (1982-87). An "X" in the "Can" column means that it is considered to be rare throughout Canada. An "X" in the "Ont" column means that it is considered to be rare in Ontario.

The "NHIC" columns give the rankings assigned by the Natural Heritage Information Center (Oldham, 1994). The "G" column is the global rank of the species, while the "S" column is the provincial rank.

"1" means that the species is extremely rare within the specified region, "2" – very rare, "3" – rare to uncommon, "4" – apparently secure but with cause for long term concern, "5" – secure. A range rank (i.e. 2-3) means that the actual rank of the plant is known to be somewhere between the two ranks but more research is still required to narrow the range down.

"COSEWIC" (1996) shows the national status assigned by the Committee on the Status of Endangered Wildlife in Canada (C.O.S.E.W.I.C.), and MNR shows the Ontario provincial status assigned by the Ministry of Natural Resources, 1996. Endangered (COSEWIC) means that the species is threatened with immediate extinction throughout all or a significant portion of its Canadian range, and vulnerable means that the species is at risk because of declining numbers, for being on the edge of its range, or for some other reason such as competition from invasive species. In Ontario species designated "endangered" are protected under the Endangered Species Act.

Genus:
Goodyera R. Brown
Rattlesnake Plantains

This genus of little orchids was named in honour of John Goodyer, a 17th century English botanist. The English name refers to the beautiful leaves, which are deep, shiny blue-green with bold splashes and lines of white or silver, reminiscent of the skin of a snake. Combined with their "plantain-like" habit and the long, slender flower spike, the term "Rattlesnake Plantain" is explained. There are about twenty-five *Goodyera* species in the world but only four occur in North America. All four of these can be found within our area. The leaves of the Rattlesnake Plantain are borne in a basal rosette hugging the ground. They are evergreen and attractive and may last for several seasons. The flower stems are, noticeably, glandular-hairy. Many rosettes in a colony will not produce flowers in any given season. The Ojibway valued them as poultices for snakebites and other medicinal uses. Rattlesnake Plantains can hybridize, but this rarely occurs in our area.

19. Menzies' Rattlesnake Plantain

Goodyera oblongifolia **Raf.** [*Epipactis decipiens*, *G. decipiens*, *G.menziesii*]

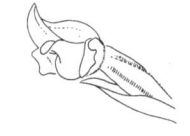

Menzies' Rattlesnake Plantain, Green Leaved Rattlesnake Plantain, Giant Rattlesnake Plantain

The species name *oblongifolia* means "oblong leaves," which distinguishes this plant from the slightly broader leaves of the other members of this genus. As for the English name, Archibald Menzies was a surgeon-naturalist on Captain James Cook's ship "Discovery" which explored the west coast of North America. Presumably, he was the first European collector of this plant in the west coast forests over two hundred years ago. Its main range is in western North America but it is semi-disjunct in the east. In Ontario it is most easily found in the Georgian Bay area.

Menzies' Rattlesnake Plantain is generally the largest and has the least-marked leaves of our Rattlesnake Plantains. It is also the commonest, particularly on the Bruce Peninsula where it is found frequently. It displays a hint of Niagara Escarpment affinity in Bruce and Grey Counties. It can be found in bloom from late July to almost the end of August, rarely later. Rattlesnake Plantain can be found in dry or moist cedar, pine or mixed forests where the deep shade of the trees above allows very little vegetation on the forest floor. Here, amid the thick duff of crumbled leaves and needles, where only a few shade tolerant plants such as *Pyrola* spp., Gaywings (*Polygala paucifolia*), or Partridgeberry (*Mitchella repens*) appear, a rosette or more probably a small colony of these striking leaves may catch your eye. They are deep shiny green with a feathered white line down the midrib and very little white on the rest of the leaves. From the middle of some rosettes rises a slender stalk bearing a loose, somewhat one-sided raceme with inconspicuous off-white flowers. The whole plant is reminiscent of certain Ladies' Tresses (*Spiranthes* spp.). In fact, this genus was once classified with them.

Description
Height ±10-25 cm.
Leaves 3-7, in a basal rosette, ±8 x 2-3 cm, smooth, oval-acuminate, mid-vein feathery white or silvery, little reticulation on rest of leaf.
Spike about 8 cm long, somewhat spiralled to one side.
Flowers greenish-white.
Sepals hairy on outside. Dorsal sepal lanceolate-deltoid, 6-10 x 3.5 mm, forming a hood with connivent petals. Lateral sepals ovate-lanceolate, acuminate, 5-8 x 3-4 mm.
Lip saccate with long beak, boat-shaped, 5-8 mm long.
Column short and inconspicuous. No spur.
Flowers: late July to late August, rarely later.
Capsules obovoid-ellipsoid, ±1 cm long.

20. Downy Rattlesnake Plantain

Goodyera pubescens (Willd.) R. Br. [*Epipactis willdenovii*]
Downy Rattlesnake Plantain

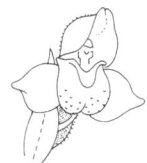

The name is from the Latin *pubescens* which means "downy" and refers to the densely pubescent inflorescence. The leaves are the most attractive and conspicuous of any in this genus. The rhizome creeps through humus, branching and elongating each year. Because of this, where it does occur, large colonies can often be found. The plants are almost as large as Menzies Rattlesnake Plantain (*Goodyera oblongifolia*). Its preferred habitat consists of any type of wooded cover with acidic surface conditions such as bogs, coniferous swamps, mixed or hardwood forests. It is mostly found on sandy soils with a good content of humus. In warm woods flowering time is earlier than in cool bogs, sometimes by as much as a month.

The Downy Rattlesnake Plantain is less boreal than the rest of the genus. Its range extends from Quebec and Ontario southward to Georgia and Alabama and westward to Minnesota. In this area it is known only from three locations in the south of the Bruce Peninsula and one southwest of Port Elgin.

Description
Height less than 30 cm. Stem is densely pubescent.
Leaves 4-8, short-petioled forming a basal rosette, 3-7 x 1-4 cm,
    oblong-elliptic, bluish-green with a prominent network of
    whitish veins forming reticulations.
Scape with 4-7 bracts lanceolate, 5-9 x 2.5 mm.
Spike cylindrical, densely flowered, up to 80 flowers.
Sepals ovate, concave, apex narrowed and blunt, white with greenish
    lateral veins, 4-5.5 x 3-4 mm.
Lateral petals connivent with dorsal sepal over column,
    oblong-spatulate, oblique, white, 5-6 x 2.5-3.5 mm.
Lip very strongly saccate, apex short, blunt, recurved, white,
    3.5-4 x 3-3.5 mm.
Column short with blunt rostellum, 2 x 2.5 mm. No spur.
Flowers: late July to September, rarely later.
Capsule globose, 6 x 6 mm.

21. Lesser Rattlesnake Plantain

Goodyera repens (L.) R. Brown var. *ophioides* Fern
[*Epipactis repens, G. ophioides*]
Dwarf Rattlesnake Plantain, Lesser Rattlesnake Plantain

As the English names suggest, this is the smallest of our Rattlesnake Plantains. The Latin "repens" refers to its "creeping" roots, and its varietal name *ophioides* means "like a snake" in reference to the leaf markings which resemble a snake skin. This is a circumboreal species with this variety being found mainly in eastern North America. Its white and green splashed leaves form a tiny rosette from the centre of which arises a delicate stem, not more than 15 cm tall. As usual with the Rattlesnake Plantains, there are many more rosettes of leaves than there are flowering plants in any one season. The raceme has gnat-sized white flowers tinged with green or brownish-pink and softly hairy on the outside. From near the end of July to the end of August, this orchid mite unfolds its diminutive beauty. It may be found in cool, shady evergreen woods or in thick moss under spruce or cedar, associated with plants such as Twinflower (*Linnaea borealis*) and the Blunt Leaf Rein Orchid (*Platanthera obtusata*). It is not very common in this area overall but is somewhat easier to find on the Bruce Peninsula where it tends to be on the Lake Huron side. The Dwarf Rattlesnake Plantain generally prefers wetter locations than other Rattlesnake Plantains and is often associated with "cold bottom" conditions.

Description
Height less than 10 cm.
Leaves 4-7, in a basal rosette, ovate, acute, often very small,
    ±2 x 0.5-2 cm, dark green with veins bordered with pale tissue
    lacking chlorophyll, forming reticulations.
Spike more or less one-sided. Flowers whitish with tiny hairs on the
    outside.
Floral bracts lanceolate, 5-12 mm long.
Dorsal sepal connivent with petals to form a hood over lip,
    ovate-oblong, 3-3.5 x 1-1.5 mm.
Lateral sepals enclosing sides of lip, ovate-oblong, 3-3.5 x 1-1.5 mm.
Lip deeply saccate with pointed beak, boat-shaped on margins.
Column short and inconspicuous. No spur.
Flowers: late July to the end of August.
Capsules ovoid, drooping, 7 x 5 mm.

22. Checkered Rattlesnake Plantain

Goodyera tesselata **Loddiges** [*Epipactis tesselata*]
Checkered Rattlesnake Plantain

Both the English and Latin names refer to the checkerboard or "tessellated" pattern of white and green on the leaves. This Rattlesnake Plantain is sometimes hard to distinguish from the others. It has paler bluish-green leaves which are usually very checkered. When seen through a magnifying glass, the lip is less deeply pouched than that of the Lesser Rattlesnake Plantain (*Goodyera repens*).

This species is found in eastern North America from Newfoundland to Manitoba and south from New England to Minnesota, our area being in the centre of its range. It usually grows in dryish conifer stands or mixed forests where conifers predominate. It is in bloom a little earlier than the other three species discussed here, approximately from mid-July to late August.

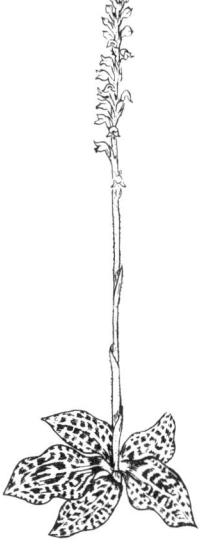

Description
Height 10-20 cm.
Leaves in a basal rosette, 2-6 x 1-2.5 cm, oblong lanceolate, pale
    blue-green usually white reticulate.
Spike a loose spiral or cylinder, approximately 3-6 cm long. Flowers
    white to greenish-white.
Hood ±5 mm lateral petals joined with dorsal sepal.
Lateral sepals hairy on outside.
Dorsal sepal elliptic-oblong, concave below, 5-6.5 x 3-3.5 mm.
Petals 5-6.5 x 2.5 mm, dilated at middle.
Lip less saccate than *G. repens* with short beak only slightly
    down-curved.
Column short and inconspicuous. No spur.
Flowers: mid-July to late August.
Capsules obovoid, erect, ±8 mm long.

Genus:
Liparis L.C. Richard
Twayblades

The botanist who named this plant chose the Greek word *liparos* from which our word "lipid" is also derived. This conveys the meaning "greasy" or "shiny" and so describes the lustre and sleek aspect of this genus. The common name demonstrates the confusion that the use of botanical (Latin) names is designed to overcome, as "Twayblade" is also commonly used in the quite different genus *Listera*. About 250 species of *Liparis* are known from temperate and tropical regions. Only two occur in Canada, of which one can be found in our two counties.

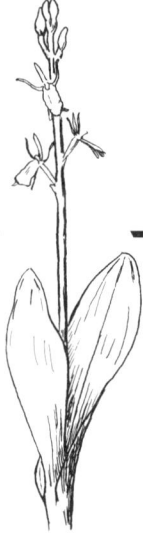

23. Loesel's Twayblade
Liparis loeselii **(L.) Richard ex Lindley**
Loesel's Twayblade, Fen Orchid, Bog Twayblade

The name of Loesel's Twayblade commemorates the German botanist Johann Loesel (1607-1655). Germany is in the middle of the plant's western European range. This inconspicuous plant grows in a variety of habitats. Its sleek green leaves and a dozen or so yellowish flowers may be seen in fens, wet sandy meadows, marly or sandy lakeshores, ditches or even moist, abandoned gravel pits. In this area, it can occasionally be found in other locations such as upland deciduous forests and old fields but it prefers rather sterile, moist conditions. The leaves are always ascending as the plants bloom. The flowers look somewhat like large specimens of White Adder's Mouth (*Malaxis monophyllos*) and give a similar gnomish impression. The variety of its habitats and its common occurrence in the Georgian Bay area would make one expect this orchid to be better known. However, it grows partly in "scrubby" wet vegetation that hides the plant and deters the orchid hunter. It is usually in flower from the last third of June into July but is often overlooked because of its association with more spectacular species blooming at the same time in these locations.

This orchid very commonly sets seed. Last year's pale seed capsules are often seen persisting beside the blooming plant of the current year. The flowers develop and fade rather quickly, further adding to the inconspicuous nature of this plant. It rarely reaches twenty centimetres in height in this area. Among the most appealing sights however, are the dwarfed forms of Loesel's Twayblade that grow on exposed shores of the Great Lakes, with one or two pert, normal sized blooms confidently perched on very delicate stems. The upturned, hairlike lateral petals are distinctive.

In North America, Loesel's Twayblade occurs mainly from the Maritimes to Manitoba, extending as far south as West Virginia and Iowa. In this area, it is fairly widespread but rather uncommon. The best chance of finding it is in the Oliphant to Howdenvale area of the Bruce Peninsula.

Description
Height 3-18 cm. Stem Smooth.
Leaves 2, glossy green, basal, oblong to oblong-lanceolate, subacute,
    keeled, 2-12 x 1-5 cm.
Raceme lax to relatively densely flowered with 1-15 blossoms.
flowers yellowish-green to greenish-white.
Sepals and petals linear with incurved margins, greenish, 5-6 x 1-2 mm,
    the petals narrower and slightly shorter.
Lip, 4-5 x 2-3 mm, cuneate-orbicular to obovate, arcuate-recurved,
    apiculate with finely crenulate margins.
Column elongate, curved, winged. No spur.
Flowers: Late June to July.
Capsules ellipsoid, ascending, ±10 x ±3 mm.

Genus:
Listera R. Brown
Twayblades

These tiny inconspicuous plants were named to honour Martin Lister, an English physician and naturalist of the late 17th century. The English name "Twayblade" refers to the two leaves which are placed more or less opposite each other halfway up the slender stem. The tiny flowers, only about the size of a mosquito in our native species, have a hanging lip which is usually cleft into variously shaped lobes at the tip. The column is erect.

Twayblades are plants of the northern hemisphere; they thrive in cold, acid situations and often grow in deep mats of Sphagnum moss. Eight species are found throughout Canada and the United States, three in the Bruce-Grey area. Although widely distributed, native Twayblades are not common anywhere and, because of their small size, they are difficult to find.

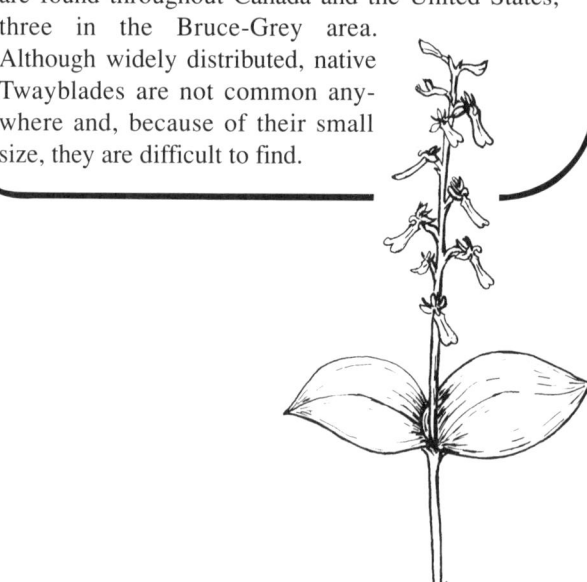

24. Broad Lipped Twayblade
Listera convallarioides (Sw.) Nutt.
Broad Lipped Twayblade, Broad Leaved Twayblade

Convallarioides means "like *convallaria*," or Lily-of-the-Valley, and may refer to the colonies of broad leaves formed by these plants. Like the Heart Leaved Twayblade (*Listera cordata*), this orchid is easily missed, even though it is a little larger and less delicate. It bears two smooth, opposite satiny-green leaves which are located just above the middle of the stem. Above the leaves is the raceme bearing up to 20 greenish-yellow flowers with long broad lips that are slightly notched at the end and narrow and toothed at the base. The miniature flowers are suspended on short stems, and thrust forward to receive any tiny insects that may visit them.

You may find Broad Leaved Twayblade in bloom in this area in late June or early July. It often grows in cedar, mixed, or deciduous swamps or less often in damp coniferous to mixed woods, usually in deep shade. The colonies may contain hundreds of plants. Accompanying species may be Naked Mitrewort (*Mitella nuda*) and Blunt Leaved Orchid (*Platanthera obtusata*). This species tends to be found in "cold bottom" conditions. It grows across the continent from Newfoundland to Alaska and southward to California and the mountains of Tennessee. South of the Bruce Peninsula, it is more common in Grey County than in Bruce.

Description
Height 5-18 cm.
Leaves 2, opposite, a little above mid-stem, ovate-elliptic to
    sub-orbicular, obtuse to acute, smooth satiny green,
    2-5 x 1-4 cm, smooth underneath, minutely downy above.
Flowers on slender pedicels in a loose raceme 2-12 cm long,
    pale, translucent yellowish-green.
Petals and sepals linear, reflexed, 4-5 mm long.
Lip 8-12 mm long, cuneate, shallowly notched at the wider apex
    with the lobes rounded, with a short triangular tooth on
    each side near the base.
Column shorter than lip, erect. No spur.
Flowers: late June to early July.
Capsules obovoid, ±1 cm long.

25. Heart Leaved Twayblade

Listera cordata (L.) R. Brown
Heart Leaved Twayblade

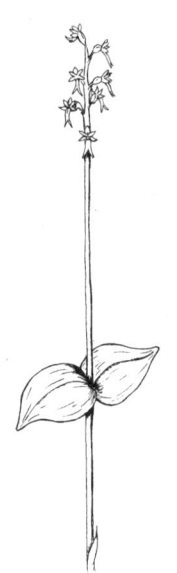

Both the English and Latin names refer to the heart-shaped form of the tiny leaves. The plant is so inconspicuous that it is possible to walk through a whole colony and not notice it at all. Look for a small green, somewhat shiny plant. The slender stem, above the two leaves, is topped with a short raceme of about eight to ten minute mauve, purple or greenish spidery flowers. The long narrow lip forks into two sharp lobes for half its length, and is somewhat thrust forward. The seed capsules behind expand and ripen as soon as the flower has been fertilized and before it withers, often giving the effect of a flower hanging from a tiny balloon.

This delicate little orchid blooms from late May to the beginning of July in our area, in sun-dappled openings in mossy coniferous and mixed forests where plants such as Twinflower (*Linnaea borealis*), Wild Lily-of-the-Valley (*Maianthemum canadense*) and various ferns are to be found. It responds well to "cold bottom" conditions. It occurs mainly on the Bruce Peninsula but can also be found in the remainder of Grey County. It is rare in both. It has not been found in Bruce County south of the Peninsula. Heart Leaved Twayblade is circumboreal, found in wet woods and *Sphagnum* bogs.

Description
Height 4.5-14 cm.
Leaves 2, opposite, ovate-cordate, attached a little below midway on the stem, shiny green above, paler underneath, 1-3 x 0.8-2.5 cm.
Slender raceme, 2-8 cm long, 6-20 flowers.
Flowers 3-5 mm long, green to reddish-purple. Bracts inconspicuous.
Sepals and lateral petals ovate, ±2 x 1 mm.
Lip linear, 2-4 mm long, cleft one half its length into 2 diverging, linear-lanceolate lobes.
Column tiny, erect. No spur.
Flowers: mid-May to the beginning of July.
Capsules ovoid, 5 mm long.

26. European Common Twayblade
Listera ovata (L.) R. Brown
European Common Twayblade

The Latin name is derived from the word *ovatus* meaning "ovate" and refers to the ovate leaves which are typical of this species. It is not known how this Eurasian species arrived in our area; certainly deliberate introduction by settlers cannot be ruled out. This vigorous orchid is widespread in a variety of habitats throughout Europe with the exception of Portugal. It extends into Siberia and the Indian subcontinent. In North America, it has, so far, been found naturalized only in the south-central part of the Bruce Peninsula and in Wellington and Oxford Counties, where it is rare. It is much larger than the native Twayblades.

Description
Height 20-60 cm.
Leaves 2, opposite, below middle of stem, yellow-green, ovate to elliptic, up to 15 x 12 cm.
Raceme stout, loosely to densely flowered with up to 100 flowers. Floral bracts 3 x 1 mm.
Flowers yellowish-green.
Dorsal sepal ovate, concave, 5 x 3 mm.
Lateral sepals ovate, oblique, 4 x 3 mm.
Lateral petals linear, 4 x 1 mm.
Lip linear, 9 x 4 mm, dilated and cleft at the apex into 2 blunt oblong lobes and with a small tooth between, acutely angled downward near the base.
Column 2 x 1.5 mm. No spur.
Flowers: June and July.
Capsule semi-erect, ellipsoid, 10 x 6 mm.

Genus: *Malaxis* Solander
Adder's Mouths

Malaxis is a Greek word that means "a softening" and refers to the texture of the sleek leaves. Approximately 200 species exist, mostly throughout tropical areas except Africa. Three species are known from Canada, two of which can be found in this area. These plants are small and inconspicuous and thus offer a great challenge to the orchid hunter.

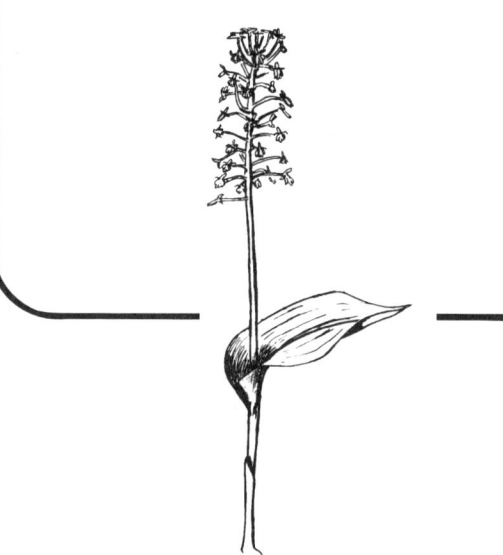

27. White Adder's Mouth

Malaxis monophyllos (L.) Swartz
var. *brachypoda* (A. Gray) Morris & Eames [*M. brachypoda*]
White Adder's Mouth

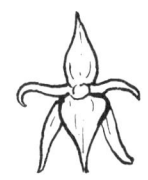

The species name for this orchid comes from the Greek words *monos* meaning "solitary" and "phyllon" meaning "leaf." Our White Adder's Mouth differs somewhat from that of Europe and has been designated a variety. The latter name comes from the Greek words *brachys* meaning "short" and *podion* meaning "foot." This refers to the short flower stalks. However, the most dramatic difference between the two varieties is the fact that on our variety the lip is in the "normal" or lowermost position, while the European variety twists its blossoms in a complete circle to place the lip uppermost.

The White Adder's Mouth has one of the tiniest blossoms of all orchids. A large plant will stretch only the length of a hand. The blossoms look like tiny, chubby elves with long tapering beards and conical caps. About 15-30 of the tiny flowers stand primly in a loose spire. In wetter cedar, balsam fir and spruce woods and in mixed to deciduous swamps, these frail orchids can be found in soggy depressions around tree bases in cool, deep shade. In this area, the flowers open from late June to July. This species is widespread but not very abundant. It becomes slightly more frequent northward on the continent and spreads across it, in the boreal forest, from Newfoundland to British Columbia and southern Alaska.

Description
Height 5-15 cm. Stem smooth, pale green and glossy.
Leaf solitary (rarely 2), sheathing lower part of stem, light green, ovate-elliptic to linear, 1.5-10 x 1-5 cm.
Raceme very slender, elongate with 15-30 flowers widely spaced. Floral bracts 1 mm long, lanceolate.
Flowers greenish-white.
Sepals linear-oblong, acuminate, 2 x 1 mm.
Lateral petals linear, acute, 1.5 mm long, thread-like.
Lip vaguely triangular, 3-lobed with lateral lobes auriculate, thickened, curved upward and the middle lobe ovate and acuminate, 2-2.5 x 1-2 mm.
Column very short, inconspicuous. No spur.
Flowers: late June to July.
Capsules obliquely ovoid, 3.5-5 mm long.

28. Green Adder's Mouth
Malaxis unifolia **Michaux** [*Malaxis bayardi*]
Green Adder's Mouth

The botanical species name of the Green Adder's Mouth is from the Latin *unifolium* meaning one leaf, although this feature alone cannot be used to distinguish it from our other species. This is one of the smallest and rarest orchid species in Bruce and Grey Counties. In this area it requires a local acid pocket and occurs in both lowlands and uplands.

All of the *Malaxis* species are distinctive with their tiny, insect-sized, greenish flowers. However, the Green Adder's Mouth is further distinguished by its flat-topped, finger-thick raceme of extremely small blooms. From late June to the beginning of August, search the elevated hummocks of *Sphagnum* or dryish stumps and logs in cedar and spruce swamps or in sterile sandy spots where grape ferns (*Botrychium* spp.) thrive – but it is so rare that if you find it, it will probably be when you are not looking for it. Although its single raceme may have fifty tiny flowers, often only three or four will produce seeds. As the plant ages, these ripening seed capsules stand out from the mass of their wilted, dishevelled, unfertilized companions.

Malaxis unifolia is indeed a plant that has attracted the attention of botanists. Luer (1975) remarks, "In the flower some fancy they see a minute, bright green viper's head, the bifid lip resembling the bared fangs of the tiny snake," while Correll (1950) observed that "In the Green Adder's Mouth, growth seems to be momentarily arrested at anthesis, but upon fertilization of the flowers and consequent setting of the fruit, vegetative growth is resumed and the leaf frequently increases noticeably in size." It is widely distributed in eastern North America and as far south as Guatemala.

Description
Height 6-20 cm. Stem bright green, erect, smooth.
Leaf solitary, sheathing the stem for nearly half its length,
    abruptly flaring, ovate-cordate to ovate-lanceolate, keeled,
    2-8 x ±3 cm wide.
Raceme cylindric, elongated in lower part. Floral bracts minute,
    awl-shaped.
Flowers rich green.
Sepals spreading, linear-oblong, 1-3 x 1 mm, often somewhat rolled.
Lateral petals thread-like, recurved, up to 3 mm long.
Lip ±3 x 3 mm, at first uppermost, becoming lowermost at maturity,
    triangular to cordate with basal auricles, tridentate apex,
    middle tooth short.
Column very short, inconspicuous. No spur.
Flowers: very late June to early August.
Capsules sub-horizontal, ellipsoid, 3-6 mm long, 2-3 mm diameter.

Genus:
Piperia Rydberg

This genus is named after Professor C. V. Piper (1867-1926), who was a plant enthusiast of the Pacific Northwest. The mountains and coasts of that area are home to the three species within this genus. Only *Piperia unalascensis* leap-frogs across the continent to the Upper Peninsula of Michigan, the shores of Lake Huron and the Gulf of St. Lawrence. These plants are characterized by two (occasionally three) fleshy, egg-shaped tubers and have leaves that usually die down before or during flowering.

29. Alaska Orchid
Piperia unalascensis (**Sprengel**) **Rydberg** [*Habenaria unalascensis*]
Alaska Orchid

The Latin name of this plant reflects its western distribution, as it is named after the Aleutian Island of Unalaska. It has sleek basal leaves and a tall, thin flower raceme which superficially resembles the Slender Ladies' Tresses. The flowers, however, are tiny and green with a short spur.

The very slender raceme of greenish flowers may grow to be knee-high, yet the blossoms are smaller than a Ladybug. The plants are fairly common throughout the four northern townships of the Bruce Peninsula, more so towards the north and west of Highway 6. South of Sauble Beach it appears to be restricted to the Lake Huron shore, where it is very rare. There has not been a confirmed report from Grey County. It may blend in with early summer grasses and sedges on dry, bushy lands, but normally can be seen in the partial or full shade of conifers such as spruces, pines or cedars. The soil will almost always be dry and thin, to virtually non-existent, over dolostone. The Alaska Orchid is a plant of early summer and can be found from late June through July along with plants such as Buffalo Berry (*Shepherdia canadensis*), Round Leaved Dogwood (*Cornus rugosa*) and mats of pink blossomed Twinflower (*Linnaea borealis*).

The Alaska Orchid is relatively common along the west coast of North America from southern Alaska to the Baja Peninsula. East of Wyoming it is known in only two areas: the central Great Lakes (including Bruce County) and Anticosti Island in the Gulf of St. Lawrence. Thus it is a classic western disjunct species. The Lake Huron shore of southern Bruce County represents the most southerly extent of its range in eastern North America. Some people believe that the eastern locations are remnants of a formerly broader distribution, which perhaps occurred at the time of the pine maximum about 7,000 to 9,000 years ago.

Description
Height 10-60 cm, averaging 20-25 cm.
Sheathing bracts at base of stem, 1 or 2.
Leaves 2 (rarely up to 4) above bracts on lower part of stem, shiny
    green to green-yellow, narrow oblanceolate to obovate, blunt,
    5-12 x 1-3 cm withering before or during flowering.
Slender spike-like raceme with numerous, unequally distributed, tiny
    flowers.
Flowers greenish-white to straw coloured, fragrant or sometimes
    malodorous.
Sepals and lateral petals 2-4 x ±1 mm wide.
Lip ovate-lanceolate, 2-4 x ±2 mm, fleshy.
Column short, inconspicuous. Spur slender, 3-4 mm long
Flowers: late June to early August, rarely in early June.
Capsules ascending, ellipsoid, 6 x 3 mm.

Genus: *Platanthera* L. C. Richard
Rein Orchids (Orchis)

The name of this genus is derived from the parts of the flower. The Greek word *platys* means "wide" and "anthera," means anther (i.e. the pollen bearing part of the stamen). This genus includes the majority of species formerly in the genus *Habenaria* and still retains a significant amount of the variability of that group. It is the most common and diverse orchid genus in temperate and boreal North America. It should be noted that the words **orchid** and **orchis** – in the English names – are often used interchangeably in this genus depending on author preference and local usage. Similarly, **leaf** is used in some books and **leaved** in others.

The common occurrence and diverse structure of these orchids have caused some botanists to propose that *Habenaria* be split into as many as thirteen genera, while most popular books recognize only one. Here, the treatment for this complex group, given in Luer (1975), is followed. In his opinion, there are 36 species and major varieties of the genus *Platanthera* in the United States and Canada. That gives this area 12 taxa (11 species, one with 2 varieties).

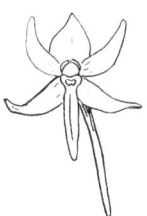

30. White Fringed Orchis
Platanthera blephariglottis (Willd.) Lindley
[*Habenaria blephariglottis*]
White Fringed Orchis

The Latin name of this species is derived from the Greek words *blepharon* meaning "eyelid" and *glotta* meaning "tongue" in reference to the finely fringed labellum which looks like a "tongue like an eyelid." This is one of the loveliest of wildflowers. It is not common but, when it is found, there are typically large numbers, sometimes even thousands, of flowers. The White Fringed Orchis grows best in the deep *Sphagnum* of open Black Spruce-Tamarack bogs which are only partially shaded by the surrounding woods. It can sometimes be found in the company of Pitcher Plant (*Sarracenia purpurea*), Large Cranberry (*Vaccinium macrocarpon*), Rose Pogonia (*Pogonia ophioglossoides*) and Grass Pink (*Calopogon tuberosus*).

The White Fringed Orchis can be found from Newfoundland west to Ontario and Michigan, south to Florida and Mississippi. It is considered rare in Ontario. In this area, it is not known on the Bruce Peninsula and is rare in the rest of Bruce and Grey Counties.

Description
Height up to 60 cm. Stem erect, leafy.
Leaves 2-3, elliptic to lanceolate, green, keeled, up to 20 x 3 cm,
    sheathing the stem below, becoming bracts above.
Raceme loosely to densely flowered, 20-30 flowers. Floral bracts
    lanceolate, 1-2 cm long. Flowers bright white.
Dorsal sepal broadly ovate, obtuse, concave, 5-8 x 4-6 mm.
Lateral sepals broadly ovate, oblique, reflexed, 5-10 x 4-9 mm.
Lateral petals narrowly oblong, denticulate or essentially entire,
    3-8 x 1.5-3 mm.
Lip ovate, fringed, 10 x 6 mm, fringes 3-6 mm long.
Column 3 x 3 mm. Spur 1.5-2 cm long.
Flowers: July and early August.
Capsule ellipsoid, 20 x 5 mm.

31. Club Spur Orchid

Platanthera clavellata (**Michaux**) **Luer** [*Habenaria clavellata*]
Club Spur Orchid, Green Woodland Orchis

Both the botanical and English names for this plant refer to the club-shaped spur which is the prominent nectary of this unassuming orchid. This plant often forms large colonies in acid situations, commonly in Black Spruce-Tamarack bogs, throughout its range which extends from the southern United States to the northern Great Lakes and Newfoundland. The Club Spur Orchid is often associated with "cold bottom" conditions. However, in this area it is rare because of the predominately limy, basic soils which do not suit this acid loving species. Even where common, this orchid is not easy to find. Luer (1975) describes the plant as "A short, broad and often somewhat dishevelled raceme of comparatively few flowers producing an inconspicuous display at the tip of the stem." The flowers often twist sideways so that they have an askew look and are green-yellow with a distinctive three-lobed lip. The plants have one grey-green leaf about halfway down the plant stem and send out rhizomes which connect dozens of plants underground.

Look for this interesting little species rising about 10-20 cm above the boggy floors of cedar or spruce woods or in *Sphagnum* openings along with plants such as Round Leaved Sundew (*Drosera rotundifolia*) and sometimes Pink Lady's Slipper (*Cypripedium acaule*). The Pink Lady's Slippers will have well developed capsules by the time the Club Spur Orchid flowers, usually during mid to late July or early August.

Description
Height 5-25 cm tall. Stem smooth.
One well-developed leaf, oblanceolate, near middle of stem,
    5-12 x 1-3 cm, other leaves reduced to linear, acute bracts.
Flowers yellowish green, 3-15 in a short terminal raceme. Flowers often
    turned sideways – up to 45°.
Dorsal sepal ovate, rounded, 4-5 x 2 mm. Lateral sepals oblique,
    4-5 x 2 mm.
Lateral petals ovate, 3-5 x 2 mm.
Lip oblong, truncate, obscurely 3-lobed, 3-7 x 3-4 mm. Spur slender
    with dilated tip, ±10 mm long. Column 1 x 1.5 mm.
Flowers: mid-July to mid-August, rarely later.
Capsules horizontal, ellipsoid, 10 x 4 mm.

32. Tall White Bog Orchid

Platanthera dilatata (**Pursh**) **Lindley ex Beck** [*Habenaria dilatata*]
Tall White Bog Orchid, Bog Orchid, Bog Candles

The Latin word *dilatata* means "expanded" and refers to the base of the lip of this orchid. English names such as "Fragrant Orchid," "Bog Candles" and "Tall White Bog Orchid" have been inspired by the pure white, clove or vanilla scented spires of blossoms that frequently stand conspicuously amongst low fen vegetation. Well grown individuals of this species are attractive and dramatic. The lovely spire of snow white blossoms contrasts with, and is complemented by, the leafy green lower stem.

The Tall White Bog Orchid is common across North America in the north and also in the mountainous west where thousands of plants may cover each acre of sunny wet terrain. In this area, it is rather uncommon but it is truly rare in Grey County. It grows up to 65 cm tall and can be found in fens, most typically marly fens very near or at the Lake Huron shoreline. It is sometimes common in these fens. It can also rarely be found in wet marly roadside ditches. The plant is often found with sedges (*Carex* spp.), Pitcher Plant (*Sarracenia purpurea*), and sundews (*Drosera* spp.). Occasionally, it is found growing with the closely related Tall Northern Green Orchid (*Platanthera hyperborea*). These two orchids bloom at about the same time, with the Tall White Bog Orchid usually in flower from June to July. The hybrid (*P.* x *media*) of these two has been reported from this area.

Description
Height 15-65 cm tall. Plant erect, glabrous.
Leaves linear to lanceolate, dark green, up to 25 x 5 cm, gradually
 reduced to bracts upwards.
Raceme lax to dense, 12-60 flowers. Flowers white. Floral bracts
 lanceolate, 3 mm long.
Dorsal sepal ovate, obtuse, with lateral petals forming a hood over
 column, 3-7 x 2-4 mm.
Lateral sepals elliptic-lanceolate, blunt to acuminate, spreading or
 reflexed, 4-9 x 1-2 mm.
Lateral petals ovate-lanceolate, falcate, 3-8 x 1.5-4 mm.
Lip 5-10 x 2-5 mm, elongate broad at base, projecting outwards but
 often recurving upwards to close flower after pollination.
Spur cylindric, approximately same length as lip. Column ±2 x ±1.5 mm.
Flowers: June to July, in at least one location as late as September.
Capsules semi-erect, ellipsoid, ±12 x ±6 mm.

33. Tubercled Orchid

Platanthera flava (**L.**) **Lindley** [*Habenaria flava*]
Tubercled Orchid

The scientific name for this plant is from the Latin word *flavus* meaning "yellow" in reference to the yellowish-green flowers. The English name refers to the projection in the middle of the lip. The Tubercled Orchid is primarily a southern plant. It can be found from Nova Scotia west to Ontario and Minnesota, south to the Appalachian Mountains, Florida and Texas. It most often grows in wet, swampy hardwood forests where shallow puddles of standing water occur in spring and after heavy rain. It either grows in such pools or, occasionally, along lake shores or in moist sandy areas. When found there are usually colonies of fifty to two hundred plants. Although flowering begins in June, the floral parts usually persist in a fresh condition on the developing capsules for several weeks. In this area, it is rare in Bruce County, where it has been found in only two general locations. It has not been found in Grey County. The leaves are shinier than in the similar Tall Northern Green Orchid (*Platanthera hyperborea*).

Description
Height 15-35 cm. Stem erect, leafy.
Leaves 1-5, mid-green shiny, lanceolate, 5-20 x 1-5 cm, sheathing the stem, becoming bracts above.
Spike lax to densely flowered with 10-40 flowers. Floral bracts lanceolate, acuminate, ±3 cm long on lower part.
Flowers yellow-green.
Dorsal sepal ovate, obtuse, concave, 4 x 2.5 mm.
Lateral sepals ovate, oblique, 4 x 2.5 mm.
Lateral petals ovate, obtuse, 4 x 3 mm, forming a hood with the dorsal sepal.
Lip oblong, rounded or obtuse, ±5 x ±3 mm, base usually has a triangular lobe on either side, with an outward projecting tubercle in the middle near the base.
Column 1.5 x 2 mm. Spur slender, clavellate, 5-7 mm long.
Flowers: mid-June through July.
Capsule semi-erect, ellipsoid, 8 x 4 mm.

34. Hooker's Orchid
Platanthera hookeri (**Torrey**) **Lindley** [*Habenaria hookeri*]
Hooker's Orchid

Although this plant is named for the famous botanist W. J. Hooker (1785-1865), Hooker's Orchid could also aptly be called the "Hooked Orchid." On seeing an open blossom one is immediately struck by the strongly upcurved, hook-tipped lip. These blossoms, one or two dozen of them, rise like a thin spire of yellow-green gargoyles above a pair of sleek green basal leaves which are about the size and shape of saucers. It is altogether a singular plant.

Its favourite haunt is dryish sandy woods (especially towards Lake Huron) with dark recesses pierced by dramatic rays of sunlight, where it catches the eye in spite of its rather drab colouring. In this area, Hooker's Orchid may be seen in flower from late May until very early July and is known to be most common and easiest to find in the Sauble Beach area. It is now even rare in Bruce and Grey Counties than formerly, with the Sauble Beach population having been greatly reduced in recent decades by development. Hooker's orchid occurs from Nova Scotia to Manitoba and south to Iowa and New Jersey.

Description
Height 18-40 cm.
Basal leaves 2, almost opposite, orbicular to elliptic, slightly arched or
 lying flat, dull light green, fleshy, 4-10 x 3-9 cm.
Spike lax, 6-40 flowers. Scape usually bractless. Floral bracts
 lanceolate, ±15 x 6 mm.
Flowers yellowish-green.
Dorsal sepal triangular, lanceolate, ±10 x 3-5 mm.
Lateral sepals reflexed against the ovary, lanceolate, oblique,
 9-14 x 3-4 mm.
Lateral petals linear, dilated at base, connivent with dorsal sepal to form
 a hood, 7-9 x 2 mm.
Lip fleshy, lanceolate to triangular, distinctly upcurved (hooked) at tip,
 9-12 x 3-4 mm. Column 3 x 3 mm.
Spur wide at the base, steadily tapering to the tip, 1.5-2 cm long.
Flowers: late May to very early July.
Capsules erect, ellipsoid, 12 mm x 5 mm.

35. Tall Northern Green Orchid
Platanthera aquilonis Sheviak
[*Platanthera hyperborea* (L.) Lindley; *Habenaria hyperborea*]

Until recently this species was called *Platanthera (or Habenaria) hyperborea*. Originally named from an Icelandic specimen; it has now been determined that *P. hyperborea* is found only in Iceland and Greenland. It is genetically different from the North American plants which have been given the new name. Although this species ranges across North America and through Alaska to Japan, some of its most vigorous forms occur on the Bruce Peninsula. These stout, robust plants tend to grow in moist to wet locations which are at least partially shaded. Many yellow-green flowers are produced on a leafy stalk which can reach a maximum height of one metre. However, most of the plants in this area are of a sparser form and these occur in dryish to very wet mixed, coniferous and deciduous woods, shady, mucky shrubbery, stream sides, lake shores and bog borders. The Tall Northern Green Orchid is common throughout this area but its inconspicuous colouring and swampy habitat make it relatively unknown. It is perhaps our most ecologically versatile orchid species.

The many small yellowish-green or green flowers are very similar to those of the Tall White Bog Orchid (*Platanthera dilatata*) except for the colour and the shape of the lip.

Description
Height ±15-80 cm. Habit variable.
Leaves several, linear-elliptic to oblanceolate-lanceolate, obtuse,
    4-25 x 1-4 cm, ascending, gradually reduced to bracts above.
Spike short or long, lax or dense, few to many flowered.
    Floral bracts lanceolate, up to 3 cm long.
Flowers green in shade, yellowish in sun.
Dorsal septal ovate-elliptic, obtuse, concave, 3-4 x ±2 mm, forming a
    hood with the lateral petals.
Lateral sepals elliptic-lanceolate, oblique, spreading or reflexed,
    3-6 x 1-3 mm.
Lateral petals ovate-lanceolate, oblique to falcate, 3-6 x 1-3 mm.
Lip elliptic to lanceolate, tapering from a slightly broader base,
    4-6 x 2-3 mm.
Spur cylindrical or slightly clavate, about as long as the lip.
Flowers: last two-thirds of June (rare earlier) to end of July or early
    August (rarely into September or October).
Capsules semi-erect, ellipsoid, 10 x 5 mm.

Platanthera huronensis **Nutt.**

First described in 1818, *Platanthera huronensis* is again being recognized as a separate species. It is distinguished by larger whitish-green flowers and a strong fragrance. It should be looked for at the edges of fens, shoreline marshes or roadside ditches crossing these areas.

Description
The description for *P. aquilonis* applies, except for the flower colour and fragrance as mentioned above.

36. Ragged Fringed Orchid
Platanthera lacera (**Michaux**) **G. Don** [*Habenaria lacera*]
Ragged Fringed Orchid

The scientific name is from the Latin word *lacera* meaning "torn" in reference to the deeply fringed lips of the flowers, to which the English name also refers. Despite the fringed lip, this is not a conspicuous flower because of its drab colouring which varies from pale yellow-green to greenish-white.

The Ragged Fringed Orchid is hardier than many of the Rein Orchids, growing in a variety of sterile acid soil situations. The amount of moisture seems unimportant, so long as the area is not completely dry. It is found frequently in *Sphagnum* bogs in the company of Cranberry (*Vaccinium* spp.), Leatherleaf (*Chamaedaphne calyculata*), Rose Pogonia (*Pogonia ophioglossoides*), Bog Rosemary (*Andromeda polifolia*) and Pitcher Plant (*Sarracenia purpurea*). However, it is seldom found in the wettest part. Sometimes it occurs in wet meadows, roadside ditches or moist fields, often in the company of Wild Strawberry (*Fragaria virginiana*), Goldenrod (*Solidago* spp.), Loesel's Twayblade (*Liparis loeselii*), and Horsetails (*Equisetum* spp.). Locally, it grows in acidic or less alkaline parts of swamps, fens or bogs. Other rare species such as Brown Beakrush (*Rhynchospora fusca*) and Creeping Sedge (*Carex chordorhiza*) may be found nearby. It has also been reported from at least one old field. It is rare in both Bruce and Grey Counties. The Ragged Fringed Orchid can be found from Nova Scotia west to Manitoba, south to Georgia and Texas.

Description
Height 20-50 cm. Stem erect, slender to stout.
Leaves 2-5, sheathing the stem, elliptic to lanceolate, keeled, lowermost up to 25 x 5 cm, becoming bracts above.
Raceme lax to dense, 20-40 flowers. Floral bracts lanceolate, ±2 cm long.
Flowers pale yellow-green to greenish-white.
Dorsal sepal ovate, 4-7 x 3-5 mm.
Lateral sepals oblong, oblique, spreading, 4-8 x 3-4 mm.
Lateral petals linear-oblong, 5-8 x 2 mm, margins sometimes dentate.
Lip ±12 x ±14 mm, tripartite, narrowed at the base. Outer lobes deeply divided into almost threadlike segments, middle lobe less divided.
Column 3 x 2 mm. Spur slender or clavellate, 14-21 mm long.
 Flowers: Late June to July, rarely later.
Capsule elliptic, ±12 x 5 mm.

37. Prairie Fringed Orchid
Platanthera leucophaea (**Nuttall**) **Lindley**
[*Habenaria leucophaea*]
Prairie Fringed Orchid or Prairie White Fringed Orchid

This plant of the wet prairies of the Mississippi Valley was once common from Louisiana to Minnesota but its habitat has been largely destroyed by farming. Now it is mostly to be found in sedgy fens and meadows of the Great Lakes region. The Latin name comes from two Greek words, *leucon* meaning white and *phoios* meaning dusky, referring to the off-white or creamy colour of the large, attractive flowers. As with all the tall *Platanthera* orchids, the leaves clasp the stem. They are green-yellow above but a paler silvery-green below. Non-flowering plants are difficult to see amongst the colonies of Hair Grass (*Deschampsia caespitosa*), Cord Grass (*Spartina pectinata*) and Twig Rush (*Cladium mariscoides*) that are commonly associated species on the Bruce Peninsula. Occasionally a plant may be seen with the top eaten off since White-Tailed Deer find it quite a delicacy.

The unusual habitat requirements make this a very rare find in Bruce and Grey Counties. It occurs on the northern Bruce Peninsula and in central Grey County in two types of habitat: lake margins and a slightly marly fen. The stems sometimes reach a height of 60 cm and can easily be seen in their open habitat – a creamy white spire shimmering in the heat waves of the bright "dog days" of July or early August. Upon closer examination, 15-25 fringe-lipped blossoms can be distinguished, each about the size of a quarter and with a long, nectar-filled spur.

Description
Height 10-60 cm, mostly less than 40 cm. Stem leafy, angled.
Leaves elliptic to lanceolate, keeled, rather acute, 8-20 cm long, 2-5 cm wide. Upper leaves smaller.
Raceme large, showy, with 15-40 (or fewer) faintly cream coloured flowers. Fragrant.
Bracts lanceolate-acuminate, 1-4 cm long.
Sepals 8-15 x 5-8 mm, green or greenish white, ovate, concave.
Lateral petals cuneate to fan-shaped, erose-toothed at the apex.
Lip 1.5-3 cm long and about as wide, deeply 3-parted, narrowed to base, each lobe deeply fringed. Column 3 x 3 mm.
Spur slender, clavellate, 2-5 cm long.
Flowers: July or early August.
Capsules ellipsoid, 18 x 9 mm.

38. Blunt Leaf Rein Orchid

Platanthera obtusata (**Banks ex Pursh**) **Lindley** [*Habenaria obtusata*]
Blunt Leaf Rein Orchid, One Leaf Rein Orchid

The single, broadly blunted leaf of this species makes it easy to identify and is the origin of both the botanical (Latin *obtusata* means blunted) and English names. This is one of the few plants known to be pollinated by mosquitos. It is widely distributed with a circumboreal range extending even beyond the northern forests into the tundra. It is rather widespread in our area but not very abundant and is considered rare in Bruce County south of the Bruce Peninsula. This species is often associated with "cold bottom" conditions. The Blunt Leaf Rein Orchid seldom grows much taller than an unsharpened pencil and is difficult to see if it is growing among higher vegetation. However, it is easier to locate in the shade of moist, dense mixed and conifer woods, with Trembling Aspen (*Populus tremuloides*), White Cedar (*Thuja occidentalis*), Balsam Fir (*Abies balsamea*), Black Spruce (*Picea mariana*) and White Birch (*Betula papyrifera*). Its lax spike of three to fifteen glistening flowers often stands above such low and trailing plants as Twinflower (*Linnaea borealis*), Starflower (*Trientalis borealis*) and Creeping Snowberry (*Gaultheria hispidula*). It flowers in late June or early July for the most part.

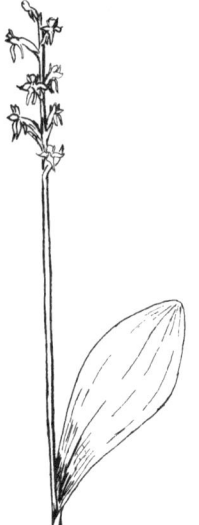

Description
Height 5-20 cm. Stem smooth, rarely has a bract.
Leaf usually single, basal, obovate to oblanceolate, obtuse and tapering
 to the base, 3-8 x 1-4 cm.
Raceme lax, flowers short-pedicelled, up to 15. Floral bracts lanceolate,
 ±10 x ±3 mm.
Flowers greenish-white.
Dorsal sepal ovate, rounded at tip, 3-5 mm long, connivent with lateral
 petals to form a hood over the column.
Lateral sepals reflexed, lanceolate-elliptic, obtuse, 4-5 x 2-3 mm.
Lateral petals lanceolate, 4-5 x 2 mm.
Lip fleshy, linear-lanceolate, 6-10 x 2 mm, dilated at the base. Spur is
 tapered, 4-8 mm long. Column 2 x 2 mm.
Flowers: mid-June to early August.
Capsules erect, elliptic, 7-10 mm long.

39. Round Leaf Orchid
Platanthera orbiculata (Pursh) Lindley
[*Habenaria orbiculata*]

Botanists have used the Latin word *orbiculata* for this plant because of its round leaves which may, when fully developed, approach the size of dinner plates. As Luer (1975) comments, "The leaves hug the ground so tightly that they even follow the contour of objects which cannot be readily pushed aside while they expand." However, the leaves of both this species and Hooker's Orchid (*P. hookeri*) are erect and small when they first emerge from the ground. In our area, this species tends to occur in moister woodlands than *P. hookeri*. However, the two plants seldom, if ever, reach the same stage of flowering in unison. Round Leaf Orchids will usually just be pushing up their spikes while the Hooker's Orchid is blooming. The white, green-tinged blossoms can be seen from late June to mid-August in this area.

This species and the Large Round Leaved Orchid have long been considered varieties of the same species. Recent research has determined that they are separate species. (Flora of North America (Vol. 26). The Round Leaf Orchid is found in Newfoundland, the Maritimes, the Appalachians, southern Quebec and Ontario and across Canada but not in the prairies. It is rare here, although it has been found in both counties as far south as the Tiverton area.

Description
Height 6-45 cm tall. Scape smooth, bracted.
Leaves 2, basal, sub-opposite, essentially flat, oblong-elliptic to
    orbicular, shiny bluish-green above, silvery below, ±10 x ±8 cm.
Raceme lax to dense with ±10 watery flowers. Floral bract
    lanceolate, 12 x 4 mm.
Flowers white, tinged with green.
Dorsal sepal sub-orbicular to truncate, erect, 4-8 x 4-8 mm.
Lateral sepals ovate, oblong, falcate, reflexed, 6-12 x 5-7 mm.
Lateral petals ovate-lanceolate, falcate, reflexed, 5-11 x 2-4 mm.
Lip linear-oblong, 9-18 x ±3 mm wide. Column 5 x 6 mm.
Spur cylindric, thickened toward tip, up to 23 mm long.
Flowers: end of June to mid-August.
Capsules erect, obovoid-ellipsoid, 10-15 x 5 mm.

40. Large Round Leaved Orchid

Platanthera macrophylla **(Goldie) P.M. Brown**
[*P. orbiculata* var. *macrophylla* (Goldie) Luer; *Habenaria macrophylla*]

The specific name is derived from the Green words *macros* meaning "large" and *phyllon* meaning "leaf" in reference to the unusually large size of the leaves, which can be more than twice as large as those of the *P. orbiculata*. The large size of the leaves is the main characteristic used to distinguish between the two species, but the Dinner Plate Orchid also has a much larger spur than the Round Leaf Orchid. Here, it tends to occur in more deciduous locations with relatively rich soil, as compared with *P. orbiculata*. It has been found in both counties but is most common in Bruce County south of the Bruce Peninsula. It is considered rare in Ontario. This species occurs from Newfoundland through the Maritimes and northern New England, southern Quebec and Ontario as far west as Northern Wisconsin.

Description
Only specific features different from var. *orbiculata* are noted here but, on average, all dimensions are larger in this variety. The figures quoted here apply to extremely large specimens.
Height up to 60 cm.
Leaves up to 20 x 15 cm.
Raceme ±20 watery flowers.
Dorsal sepal up to 8 x 10 mm.
Lateral sepals up to 16 x 9 mm.
Lateral petals up to 13 x 4 mm.
Lip up to 24 mm long. Spur up to 40 mm long.
Flowers: Late June to early August.

41. Small Purple Fringed Orchid

Platanthera psycodes (**L.**) **Lindley** [*Habenaria psycodes*]
Small Purple Fringed Orchid

This beautiful flower grows to about the same height as the Prairie White Fringed Orchid (*Platanthera leucophaea*), but has smaller flowers which are about the size of a dime. Their lilac-lavender spires provide a colourful accent amongst the bright green foliage of low, wet areas. The lip is deeply three-parted and daintily fringed, often with a delicate pale or white spot at the base. The Small Purple Fringed Orchid attracts butterflies and other pollinating insects which, in turn, bring predatory spiders. You will notice shining spider threads amongst the flowers, if not the spider itself lurking in the depths of the raceme.

The plant flowers from June in the mountains of Kentucky and Tennessee, to as late as August in Newfoundland and the northern Great Lakes region. Look for it in our area from late June to early August. It is fairly common in this region. It is found in deciduous to mixed (often shrubby) swamplands, wet open meadows, or mucky soil along smaller streams or grassy roadside ditches.

Description
Height 15-50+ cm.
Leaves dull, dark to medium apple green, elliptic-oblong to
 oblong-obovate, 5-20 x 2-7 cm, reduced to bracts above.
Raceme lax to dense with 20-40 flowers – from pale to deep purple.
Sepals oblong-elliptic to ovate, 5-6 x 3-4 mm.
Lip tripartite, divisions cuneate, margins shallowly fringed,
 7-12 x 8-15 mm, narrowed at base.
Column short. Spur slender, clavellate, 12-18 mm long.
Flowers: late June to early August.
Capsules ellipsoid, 16 x 6 mm.

Genus:
Pogonia Jussieu

The Latin name comes from the Greek word *Pogon* meaning "beard" and refers to the intricately fringed lips which do resemble beards, especially when contrasted with the sleek sepals and lateral petals. Another characteristic of this small group is their fibrous root systems which can act as stolons and produce new plants which form small colonies. This genus contains approximately ten species but only one occurs in North America.

42. Rose Pogonia
Pogonia ophioglossoides (Linnaeus) **Jussieu**
Rose Pogonia, Snake Mouth, Goldcrest

The lovely Rose Pogonia received its species name from the similarity of its single sleek leaf to that of the Adder's Tongue Fern (*Ophioglossum*). This analogy to snakes was carried to an extreme by Thoreau, who wrote in 1884 that the flower "smells exactly like a snake." On the other hand, one of the English names refers to the lovely hue of the blossoms. Many enthusiasts disagree with Thoreau and find that the flowers have a delicate raspberry odour.

In late June, the Rose Pogonias begin to open their one or two flowers, each with a dark pink or red fringed lip, the centre packed with yellow bristles. The flowers perch delicately on the frail, hand-high, purple-green stem, waving in full bloom for only about five days. It is fortunate that all plants do not start flowering at once so blooms may be found throughout much of July.

This plant is said to favour acid situations such as open bogs. However, in this area, colonies occur in more calcareous, unforested wetlands (fens) or even marly meadows, particularly along the Lake Huron shoreline but also in other locations. It is uncommon overall and rare in Grey County but is often abundant where it does occur. Frequently associated plants are Grass Pink (*Calopogon tuberosus*), Pitcher Plant (*Sarracenia purpurea*), Sundews (*Drosera* spp.) and Sedges (*Carex* spp.). Its range is from Newfoundland to Minnesota south to Florida and Texas.

Description
Height 6-20 cm tall. Stem erect, slender, smooth, green to
    brownish-green.
Leaf solitary (rarely 2 to several), long-stemmed blades, 1-8 x 0.4-2 cm,
    about middle of stem.
flowers usually 1 (rarely 2-3), terminal.
Flower dark to rose pink, rarely white, fragrant.
Petals more obtuse than sepals, flushed rose pink, 1.5-2 cm long.
Lip spatulate, narrowing to tightly packed yellowish bristles at base,
    pink with dark fringed crests and lacerate toothed apical
    margin, 2-3 cm long. Column elongate, club shaped. No spur.
Flowers: late June to early August.
Capsule erect, ellipsoid, 2 cm long.

Genus:
Spiranthes L. C. Richard
Ladies' Tresses

Many species of this attractive genus occur throughout the world. The scientific name comes from the Greek words *speira* meaning "coil" and *anthos* meaning "flower," referring to the way the flowers of the raceme spiral around the stem. The name "Ladies' Tresses" refers to the resemblance of the flower spike to a braid of hair. In this area, *Spiranthes*, or Ladies' Tresses, is another group of those smaller orchids which can easily be overlooked, but which, when found, will reward the searcher with modest beauty and delicate fragrance. Six species are found in this area. This is our most difficult genus with respect to species identification

43. Case's Ladies' Tresses
Spiranthes casei **Catling & Cruise** Case's Ladies' Tresses

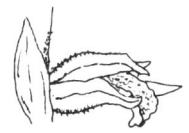

This species was separated in 1974 by P. Catling and J. Cruise and named after Fredrick W. Case II, author of "Orchids of the Western Great Lakes Region." This orchid was previously considered to be a variety of *Spiranthes cernua*. It is found in dry to moderately moist sandy, sterile soils, crevices in igneous rocks, roadsides and pastures, often with Trembling Aspen (*Populus tremuloides*), Birch (*Betula* spp.), Sumac (*Rhus* spp.) and Bracken (*Pteridium aquilinum*). It may appear in ditches, although it is more often found under drier conditions. On rare occasions it may even be found on dry sandstone ledges and bluffs. Case's Ladies' Tresses is mostly a colonizer of disturbed sites, developing large colonies then waning rapidly as conditions are modified.

Its primary habitat is the rocks and soils of the Canadian Shield, which limits the suitable locations available in this area. Consequently, it has only been found on the Bruce Peninsula at one location in Keppel Township (Grey County) in an acid pocket over dolostone in upland deciduous forest, with other rare orchids. Its range stretches from the Maritimes into Quebec, New England, Michigan and Wisconsin.

Description
Height up to 40 cm, much less in our known colony. Stem pubescent.
Basal leaves ovate-lanceolate, up to 7 x 2 cm, the lowermost withering before or at anthesis.
Sheath leaves persistent into flowering, oblanceolate to linear-oblanceolate, 12-20 x 0.5-1 cm, reduced to bladeless sheaths above.
Spike elongate, 6-15 cm long, many flowers in a loose single spiral.
Floral bracts ovate to lanceolate, long tapering, acuminate, 8-12 mm long, basally pubescent.
Flowers cream-coloured. Reddish pubescence on back.
Dorsal sepal directed forward, very slightly upturned, 5-7 mm long. Lateral sepals 5-7 x 2 mm.
Petals 5-7 mm long, with 3 distinct veins, scarcely reflexed.
Lip 6-7 x 4-5 mm, ovate, both sides may be pubescent. No spur.
Flowers: mid-August to mid-September.
Capsule ellipsoid, 10 x 6 mm.

44. Nodding Ladies' Tresses
Spiranthes cernua (L.) Rich.
Nodding Ladies' Tresses

The scientific name of this species is from the Latin *cernuus* meaning "facing the ground" and refers to the nodding position of the flowers, which is also the source of the English name. This species is most familiar in the Great Lakes region. It used to contain several varieties which have recently been separated into distinct species. These include *S. casei* and *S. magnicamporum*.

The Nodding Ladies' Tresses can be found in almost any type of open, moist area with neutral or slightly acidic soils. In this area, it prefers moist, sandy, marly soils and avoids clay. It is most prominent along lake shores, in damp meadows, pastures, roadside ditches, open marly fens, recent excavations and even lawns. Its habitat ranges from Nova Scotia west to South Dakota, south to Florida and Texas. It is found in a number of places in Bruce County but is rare in Grey County.

Description
Height up to 39 cm. Stem pubescent with blunt hairs.
Leaves 3-6, basal, green, linear-oblanceolate, relatively soft,
　　　5-23 x 0.5-2 cm, becoming bracts above.
Spike slender to stout with up to 60 flowers, 3-ranked.
Floral bracts lanceolate, acuminate, 5-15 x 3-5 mm.
Flowers white with yellowish centre, slightly nodding.
Sepals white, lanceolate with lateral sepals slightly oblique,
　　　up to 11 x 1-3 mm.
Lateral petals white, lanceolate, slightly falcate, up to 11 x 1-3 mm.
Lip white with greenish-yellow centre, ovate, constricted at the centre,
　　　up to 12 x 3-6 mm.
Column green, 4 mm long, the anther dorsal and yellow-brown with
　　　one pair of mealy pollinia. No spur.
Flowers: late August and September, or until the first heavy frost.
Capsule ellipsoid, 10 x 6 mm.

45. Northern Slender Ladies' Tresses

Spiranthes lacera (**Raf.**) **Raf.** [*Spiranthes gracilis*]
Northern Slender Ladies' Tresses, Slender Ladies' Tresses

This, as its English names observe, is the slenderest and most delicate of our Ladies' Tresses. The Latin *lacera* means "torn" and refers to the end of the lip, which is somewhat ragged. In order to see details like this in such tiny flowers, a magnifying glass is necessary.

The aspect of these little plants when in bloom is of a dainty wand on the forest floor, topped with a long spiral of pearly-white droplets. The basal leaves may fade just before or at the time of blooming. Through the lens, the flowers are seen to be waxy-white, almost translucent, little tubes formed from the dorsal sepal, the lateral petals and the lip. The lip, with its ragged tongue, has a central spot of clear bright green.

This plant ranges from the Maritimes to Manitoba and south throughout the eastern United States. In this area, it seems to be confined to the Bruce Peninsula, although it could be discovered elsewhere. Though not considered rare or very uncommon, it is not very widespread overall, as it tends to need acid conditions. The blooming period is usually from the last half of July to well into August. It can be found in rather dry, lightly shaded openings under Jack Pine, Red Pine, or other conifers. Often, it is found associated with the pink and white blooms of *Pyrola* spp. or Prince's Pine (*Chimaphila umbellata*).

Description
Height ± 12-25 cm (maximum 35 cm).
Leaves 2-5, basal, smooth shiny green, broadly oval to elliptic,
    1-4 x 1-2 cm, usually fading at or during flowering.
Slender spike a one-ranked spiral. Flowers crystalline white.
Sepals, 4 mm long. Dorsal sepal elliptic-oblong, joined to lateral petals.
Petals, 4 mm long, linear, obtuse to sub-acute.
Lip oblong, about 5 mm long, with a central green spot,
    apex fringed or ragged.
Column inconspicuous, anther on back. No spur.
Flowers: mid July to late August, rarely to October.
Capsules ascending, elliptic-avoid, 5 x 2 mm.

46. Shining Ladies' Tresses
Spiranthes lucida (H. H. Eaton) Ames
Shining Ladies' Tresses, Wide Leaved Ladies' Tresses

The English name is simply a translation of the Latin *lucida* and refers to the glossy leaves. It is a sturdier plant than the Slender Ladies' Tresses (*S. lacera*) but the flowers are more conspicuous and of an opaque whiteness. The lip of the flower is yellow with white edges, a good characteristic for identification. The raceme springs from three or more shining, relatively wide leaves. Although a distinctive flower, it is less often found than most other Ladies' Tresses partly because of its tiny size. In this area, it normally occurs on calcareous, rocky or sandy open areas, along inland lakes and rivers and Lake Huron. Often it is among grasses and sedges (*Carex* spp.) where the ground has been flooded in the spring. Some sites are fens or calcareous meadows. It is considered rare in Bruce and Grey Counties, but its range extends from New Brunswick to Michigan, and south to Virginia and Kansas.

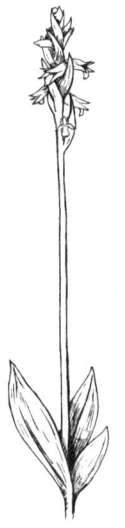

Description
Height 4-35 cm.
Leaves several, 3-10 x 0.5-2.0 cm, clustered at base, shiny green and prominent, oblong-lanceolate, blunt to acuminate. Stem leaves reduced and scale-like.
Flowers white, 1-2 or more ranks, spirally twisted around a slender spike 2-5 cm long. Stem glandular hairy.
Sepals and lateral petals linear, ±5 x 1-2 mm. Dorsal sepal with lateral petals forms a hood over the column.
Lateral sepals flank lip.
Lip ±5 x ±2 mm, edges white, median stripe yellow, oblong, rounded at the flaring apex.
Column clasped by the lip. No spur.
Flowers: mid-June to mid-July.
Capsules divergent, ellipsoid, 5 x 2 mm.

47. Great Plains Ladies' Tresses

Spiranthes magnicamporum Shev.
Great Plains Ladies' Tresses, Prairie Ladies' Tresses

The scientific name for this species is derived from the Latin words *magnus* meaning "large" and *campus* meaning "plain," a reference to the Great Plains of the mid-west which form its centre of distribution. This species was separated in 1973 from *S. cernua*. Basic soils are required but moisture does not seem to be a limiting factor as it grows on a wide range of unshaded habitats, from very dry grasslands, marshy areas which become dry in the summer, moist prairie soils with a high humus content to drier parts of marl fens. In general, it is found in drier sites than those occupied by *S. cernua*, such as natural shorelines, cobbled areas, dune ridges and prairies. It is even able to colonize sandy areas, roadsides, fallow fields and other mildly disturbed habitats. Its range includes the prairies and grasslands of the eastern Great Plains region from Texas north to North Dakota, as well as Minnesota, Illinois, Michigan and southwestern Ontario. In this area, it is very rare, having been found only at three open, treeless sites in the south-central portion of the Bruce Peninsula, of which two are clearly calcareous. Possibly it is a relict from a former climate and vegetation. It is considered a rare plant in Ontario and is the last orchid to come into bloom in this area.

Description
Height 10-30 cm tall. Stem pubescent among flowers, smooth below.
Leaves 14 x 1.2 cm, linear-lanceolate, withering early.
Spike densely spiralled with several vertical ranks. Floral bracts ovate, attenuate; 1-3 cm long.
Flowers whitish to pale cream-coloured, fragrant with a vanilla/almond scent.
Sepals linear-lanceolate, 7-11 x 1.5-3 mm.
Lateral petals linear, adherent to dorsal sepal, 7-11 x 1-2 mm.
Lip oblong-ovate, 7-11 x 3-6 mm, apex reflexed, margin crisped, centre fleshy and yellowish.
Column 3 mm long. No spur.
Flowers: from late September to October.
Capsule elliptic, 10 x 6 mm.

48. Hooded Ladies' Tresses

Spiranthes romanzoffiana **Cham.**
Hooded Ladies' Tresses

This little orchid was named in honour of Romanzoff, a Russian count and patron of the sciences. He was responsible for the exploration of the coast of Alaska. Of all the Ladies' Tresses, this is the most common in this area and is widespread in boreal and cool temperate regions of North America. Curiously, it is also found in scattered sites in the western British Isles.

This species has grass-like leaves, much narrower than in the similar species *S. cernua* and *S. magnicamporum*. The pearly white or creamy, fragrant flowers form a raceme. The lip, when examined through a magnifying glass, is somewhat fiddle-shaped and curls outward and backward from the hood above it, the latter being formed from the sepals and petals. The flowers are narrower than in *S. cernua* and spiral around the stem in three ranks and noticeably project at an angle of 45°.

In this area, Hooded Ladies' Tresses is to be found in bloom from the last half of July to early September, occasionally later. It is quite common in the northern part of the Bruce Peninsula, somewhat less so elsewhere. It prefers sunny, often marly, places, tending to grow in areas that are at least slightly flooded earlier in the season, or that have been flooded within very recent years. Sometimes colonies of hundreds of these spiral spikes can be found hidden among such plant companions as grasses, horsetails (*Equisetum* spp.), Marsh Arrowgrass (*Triglochin palustre*), sedges (*Carex* spp.), and mosses. The more dramatic spires of the Tall White Bog Orchid (*Platanthera dilatata*) will be seen in some of the same locations.

Description
Height ±7-25 cm.
Leaves 3-6, 4-20 x 0.5-1.2 cm, linear to oblong-lanceolate, smooth, mostly basal becoming smaller higher up the stem, sometimes fading at flowering.
Floral bracts thin, acuminate, 1-2.5 cm long.
Spike 3 ranked, dense.
Flowers tubular, white or creamy, fragrant.
Petals and sepals connivent forming a hood over the lip.
Sepals oblong-lanceolate, 6-13 x 3-4 mm. Petals linear, 6-12 x 1-2 mm.
Fiddle-shaped lip 9-10 x 4 mm, base concave, the free end spade-shaped and upturned.
Column inconspicuous. No spur.
Flowers: mid July to early September, occasionally later.
Capsules ovoid, erect, 10 x 4 mm.

GLOSSARY

Acuminate	– Tapering to a gradual point, the margins concave near the tip.
Acute	– Terminating in a sharp or well-defined angle of less than 90°.
Adherent	– Clinging together.
Alternate	– Of leaves borne alternately on the stem, not opposite one another.
Attenuate	– Gradually tapering to a narrow point.
Anther	– The male, pollen producing organ of the flower.
Anthesis	– The period during which a flower is open.
Apex	– The tip or end point of a leaf, bract or stem.
Apiculate	– Ending abruptly in a sharp point.
Arcuate	– Moderately curved or arching.
Ascending	– Rising somewhat obliquely or curving upward.
Auricle	– An ear-shaped appendage or lobe at the base of a leaf, bract or petal.
Auriculate	– Having auricles.
Basal	– Situated at the base.
Beak	– A firm prolonged slender tip.
Bifid	– Deeply cut in two e.g. a bifid lip
Bog	– A wet acid peatland which is poor in nutrients and is usually dominated by *Sphagnum* moss. – Usually unforested.
Boreal	– Of the North.
Bract	– A specialized leaf-like or scale-like appendage which is differentiated from the leaves in size, shape or texture and is usually found at the base of a flower or inflorescence.
Calcicole	– A species adapted to basic areas of above average pH derived from a high calcium content.
Callus	– A mass of proliferating cells, usually a solid protuberance.
Capsule	– A dry dehiscent fruit composed of more than one carpel (section).
Carpel	– The female reproductive leaf of a flower which bears the ovules. One or more forms the pistil including the ovary from which the fruit later develops.
Ciliate	– Fringed with hairs (cilia) on the margin.
Circum-	– A prefix signifying around or circling.
Clasping	– Partially surrounding another organ at the base.
Clavate	– Thickened at the end, club-shaped.
Clavellate	– Diminutive of clavate i.e. a very small club
Claw	– A narrow stalk-like part of a floral segment, generally of a petal, in orchids also of the lip.
Cleft	– Deeply cut.
Column	– In orchids, the united style and filaments which hold both male and female organs.
Connivent	– Converging but not uniting.
Cordate	– Heart-shaped.
Corm	– The enlarged fleshy base of the stem which stores food, bulb-like but solid.
Corolla	– The collective name for the petals.

Crenulate	– With rounded teeth on the margin.
Cuneate	– Narrowly triangular with the acute angle downward – from the Latin word for "wedge."
Dehisce	– The splitting open of dry fruits, anthers, etc. at maturity discharging their contents.
Deltoid	– Shaped like a triangle with equal sides – from the Greek letter *delta*.
Dentate	– Toothed, usually with teeth directed outward.
Disc	– In orchids, the upper surface of the lip.
Divergent	– Inclining away from each other.
Dolostone	– Composed largely of dolomite [Magnesium calcium carbonate – $MgCa(CO_3)_2$]. Slightly harder and more resistant to weathering than pure limestone (Calcium carbonate). Colour is similar to that of limestone.
Dorsal	– At the back or the upper surface of an organism.
Downy	– Pubescent with fine and soft hairs.
Ellipsoid	– A solid of which all plane sections through one axis are ellipses and in the plane at right angles all sections are circles.
Elliptic	– With the form of an ellipse.
Elongate	– Long and narrow.
Embryo	– The rudimentary plantlet within the seed.
Entire	– A leaf edge without toothing or division.
Epiphytic	– Growing on another plant but not parasitic.
Erect	– Growing upwards, may be inclined from the vertical.
Erose	– With a margin that appears irregular or gnawed.
Falcate	– Curved, flat and gradually tapering, scythe-shaped.
Fen	– An open area with slowly moving water and low vegetation growing on a non-acid substrate.
Filament	– The part of the stamen that supports the anther.
Genus	– A group of related species with common characteristics distinguishing them from others in the same family.
Glabrous	– Smooth, having a surface without hairs or projections.
Glandular	– A surface bearing secretory glands.
Globose	– Shaped like a sphere or a ball.
Habit	– General appearance or manner of growth of a plant.
Herbaceous	– Plants with above ground parts that die back every year.
Inferior Ovary	– The ovary is located below the perianth.
Inflorescence	– The flower-bearing shoot of a plant, may have leafy bracts associated with the flowers but not true leaves on the axis.
Involute	– Rolled inward.
Keel	– A central dorsal ridge.
Labellum	– The lip of an orchid flower, a petal generally different from the others in size, shape or colour.
Lacerate	– Irregularly cleft as if torn.
Lamella	– A thin flat plate or laterally flattened ridge.
Lanceolate	– Several times longer than wide, broadest toward the base and narrowed to the apex, lance-shaped.

Lateral	– Belonging to or borne on the sides.
Lax	– Flowers loosely spaced on spike or raceme – opposite of dense.
Linear	– Long and narrow with parallel margins.
Lip	– The third petal in orchids, usually the lowermost, often very different in size, shape and colour from the lateral petals.
Lobe	– Any segment of any organ, especially if rounded.
Malodorous	– Having an offensive odour.
Marl	– A soil or earthy deposit consisting of sand and/or clay with a very high calcium carbonate content, often found in shallow lakes or fens.
Midrib	– The central or main vein of a leaf.
Monocotyledon	– The group of plants with only one embryonic seed-leaf or cotyledon. Usually with parallel-veined leaves (as in Orchids) as opposed to net-veined leaves as in Dicotyledons (which have two seed leaves).
Nectary	– Any place or organ where nectar is secreted.
Ob-	– A prefix signifying inversion e.g. an obovate leaf is wider at the free end; an ovate leaf would be wider at the stalk end.
Oblanceolate	– broadest above the middle, tapering to the base, much longer than wide.
Oblong	– Longer than wide, with nearly parallel sides.
Obtuse	– Blunt or rounded at the end.
Opposite	– Leaves, etc. borne in pairs.
Orbicular	– Circular.
Oval	– Broadly elliptical.
Ovary	– The female or egg producing organ of the pistil.
Ovate	– An oval leaf shape with the broadest part near the stalk. Egg-shaped.
Ovoid	– A solid with an ovate outline.
Pedicel	– The short stem of a single flower in a raceme.
Peduncle	– A primary flower stalk, supporting either a cluster or a single flower.
Pendant	– Hanging or declined.
Perennial	– A plant that lives for more than 2 years. (Biennial lives two years).
Perianth	– A collective name for the sepals and petals.
Petals	– The inner ring of flower parts inside the sepals, often colourful.
Petiole	– The stalk of a leaf.
Pistil	– The female organ of the flower consisting of the stigma, style and ovary.
Plicate	– Folded lengthwise like a fan.
Pollen	– The grains formed in an anther and normally deposited on the stigma where they transmit male cells to the female ovary.
Pollinium	– A coherent mass of pollen. (Plural: pollinia)
Protocorm	– The first underground stem of a plantlet from which roots, stems, leaves, etc. arise.
Puberulent	– Covered with very tiny hairs, downy.
Pubescent	– Covered with hairs.
Quadrate	– Nearly square in form.
Raceme	– An inflorescence of many flowers, each stalked on an unbranched stem.
Ranked	– With a numerical prefix indicating the number of longitudinal rows in which leaves or flowers etc. are arranged.

Reflexed	– Bent backwards.
Resupinate	– Inverted by the twisting of the pedicel, changing the position of the flower parts as in orchids. Literally "upside down."
Reticulate	– Netted, usually a network of veins in a leaf.
Rhizome	– An underground creeping stem bearing numerous adventitious roots at the nodes and from which an erect stem bearing leaves or flowers arises.
Root	– The descending vascular axis of the plant, absorbing moisture and nutrients and providing anchorage.
Rosette	– A cluster of leaves or other organs in a circular form.
Rostellum	– A slender extension of the stigma of an orchid, which takes part in pollen transfer.
Saccate	– Sac-like or dilated.
Saprophyte	– A plant that grows on decaying vegetable matter.
Scale	– Any small thin flat structure.
Scape	– A peduncle with one or more flowers arising from the ground or a very short stem, leafless or with bracts.
Scapose	– Arranged or borne on a scape.
Scarious	– Dry and membranous in texture, generally translucent.
Secund	– Arranged or curved to lie on one side of an axis, usually applied to flowers.
Sepal	– One of the floral leaves of the outermost whorl of the flower parts.
Sessile	– Without a petiole or any other type of stalk.
Sheath	– A tubular envelope, often around the base of stems.
Solitary	– Only one.
Spatulate	– Shaped like a spatula or a rounded knife blade.
Species	– A number of similarly constructed individuals capable of interbreeding.
Spike	– An inflorescence of many sessile flowers on an unbranched stem.
Spur	– A hollow sac-like or tubular extension of some part of a flower; in orchids, the base of the lip, usually containing nectar at its distal (unattached) end.
Stamen	– The male organ of a flower, composed of a fertile anther and a sterile filament.
Staminode	– A sterile stamen or a stamen structure without an anther. Part of the column.
Stem	– A major transport and support organ of plants, as distinct from leaf, root, etc.
Stigma	– The part of the female organ of the flower that receives the pollen; usually sticky.
Stolon	– A horizontal basal shoot above ground that takes root and produces new plants.
Style	– The stalk-like part of a pistil connecting the ovary and stigma.
Sub-	– A prefix meaning below or lower.
Subulate	– Awl-shaped, narrowly triangular and tapering to a sharp point.
Succulent	– Having thick, fleshy leaves and stem.
Symbiosis	– The living together of dissimilar organisms with benefit to both.

Symmetrical	– An object that can be divided into two identical parts through a vertical plane. Radial symmetry produces two equal parts through any plane e.g. a Buttercup. Bilateral symmetry – two equal parts can only be produced through one plane e.g. an orchid.
Temperate	– Referring to climate, not liable to excessive heat or cold.
Testa	– The outer seed coat.
Tri-	– A prefix meaning three or thrice.
Truncate	– Ending abruptly, as if cut off transversely.
Undulate	– With a wavy surface or margin.
Vein	– Threads of vascular tissue in a leaf, conducting water and nutrients in solution.
Whorl	– A group of organs, such as leaves, arranged spoke-like around a central point on an axis.

REFERENCES

Argus, G. W. et al. 1982-1987. **Atlas of the Rare Vascular Plants of Ontario**. National Museum of Canada.

Bernabo, J. C. and T. Webb III. 1976. **Changing Patterns in the Holocene Pollen Record of Northeastern North America: A Mapped Summary**. Am. Quaternary Ass. Abstracts, 4th Meeting, Arizona State U.

Brown, D. M., G. A. McKay and L. Chapman. 1980. **The Climate of Southern Ontario**. Environment Canada Climatological Studies # 5.

Brown, J. R. 1985. **Flowering Dates of Orchids of the Bruce Peninsula**. The Plant Press, Vol. 3, No. 2.

Bruce-Grey Plant Committee. 1995. **A Checklist of Vascular Plants for Bruce and Grey Counties, Ontario**. Owen Sound Field Naturalists.

Burden, E. and J. H. McAndews. 1973. **A Vegetational and Geographical History Study of Methodist Point Park Reserve**. Ontario Ministry of Natural Resources.

Case, F. W. 1987. **Orchids of the Western Great Lakes Region, Revised Edition**. Cranbrook Institute of Science.

Catling, P. M. and R. E. Whiting. 1976. **Ontario's Endangered Orchids**. Ontario Naturalist, Vol. 16, #3.

Chapman, L. J. and D. F. Putnam. 1966. **The Physiography of Southern Ontario**. Univ. of Toronto Press.

Clark, Lewis J. 1973. **Wildflowers of British Columbia**. Gray's Publishing Ltd, Sidney, British Colombia.

Committee On the Status of Endangered Wildlife In Canada (C.O.S.E.W.I.C.). 1996. **1996 Canadian Species at Risk**. World Wildlife Fund.

Committee On the Status of Species At Risk in Ontario (C.O.S.S.A.R.O.). 1996. **Vulnerable, Threatened, Endangered, Extirpated or Extinct Species of Ontario**. Ontario Ministry of Natural Resources.

Correll, D. S. 1950. **Native Orchids of North America, North of Mexico**. The Cronica Botanica Co.

Eliott, H. V. 1962. **The Bruce Peninsula**. F. O. N. Bulletin #97.

Fernald, M. L. 1950. **Gray's Manual of Botany**. D. Van Nostrand Co.

Folkes, P. 1973. **The History of the Bruce Peninsula: An Overview**. Ontario Ministry of Natural Resources.

Fox, W. S. 1952. **The Bruce Beckons**. Univ. of Toronto Press.

Gibson, H. W. 1905. **Our Native Orchids**. Doubleday, Page & Co.

Gleason, H. 1968. **The New Britton & Brown Illustrated Flora**. Hafner Publishing Co.

Gleason, H. and Cronquist, A. 1991. **Manual of Vascular Plants of the Northeastern United States and Adjacent Canada**. New York Botanical Garden.

Harrington, H. D. and L. W. Durrell. 1957. **How to Identify Plants**. The Small Press Inc.

Hultén, Eric. 1968. **Flora of Alaska and Neighboring Territories**. Stanford University Press.

Humbolt, A. von. 1850. **Views of Nature**. Henry G. Bohn.

Johnson, J. 1990. **Vascular Flora of Three Regions Comprising Bruce and Grey Counties, Ontario, With Emphasis on Rare Taxa**. Ontario Ministry of Natural Resources.

Karrow, P. F., et al. 1975. **Stratigraphy, Paleontology and Age of Lake Algonquin Sediments in Southwestern Ontario, Canada.** University of Washington.

Krotkov, P. V. 1940. **Botanical Explorations in the Bruce Peninsula, Ontario.** Transactions of the Royal Canadian Institute, #9, Vol. 23, Part 1.

Luer, Carlyle A. 1975. **Native Orchids of the United States and Canada.** New York Botanical Garden.

Morris, F. and E. Eames. 1929. **Our Wild Orchids.** Charles Scribner & Sons.

Morton, J.K. and Venn, J. 1990. **A Checklist of the Flora of Ontario.** Biology Series No. 34 University of Waterloo.

Newcomb, Lawrence. 1977. **Newcomb's Wildflower Guide.** Little, Brown and Co.

Oldham, M. J. 1994. **Rare Vascular Plants.** Ontario Natural Heritage Information Centre.

Ministry of Natural Resources. 1983. **Owen Sound District and Land Office Guidelines.** M. N.R.

Peterson, R. T. and M. McKenny 1968. **A Field Guide to Wildflowers of Northeastern and North Central North America.** Houghton Mifflin Co.

Phillips, D. W. and J. A. W. McCulloch. 1972. **The Climate of the Great Lakes Basin.** Environment Canada, Climatological Studies, No. 20.

Putnam, D. F. and L. J. Chapman. 1938. **Southern Ontario Climate.** Scientific Agriculture, Vol. 28.

Szczawinski, A. F. 1975. **The Orchids of British Columbia.** British Columbia Prov. Museum, Handbook #6.

Thomson, G. W. 1970. **Vascular Plants of the Bruce Peninsula: A Review, with Comments and Additions.** The Michigan Botanist, Vol. 9, #1.

Wherry, E. T. 1948. **Wildflower Guide: Northeastern and Midland United States.** Doubleday & Co. Inc. and The American Garden Guild Inc.

Whiting, R. E. and P. M. Catling. 1986. **Orchids of Ontario: An Illustrated Guide.** The CanaColl Foundation.

Woodford, J. and G. M. Bartman. 1966. **A Garden Northward.** The Ontario Naturalist, Vol. 4, #1.

ADDITIONAL REFERENCE

Flora of North America North of Mexico. Volume 26, 2002. Oxford University Press.

Index of Names

Adam and Eve 18
Adder's Mouth
   Green 72
   White 71
Alaska Orchid 74
Amerorchis rotundifolia 16
Aplectrum hyemale 18
Arethusa 20
Arethusa bulbosa 20
Blunt Leaf Rein Orchid 84
Bog Orchid (Bog Candles) 78
Broad Lipped Twayblade 67
Calopogon
   pulchellus 22
   tuberosus 22
Calopogon 22
Calypso 24
Calypso bulbosa 24
Club Spur Orchid 77
Coeloglossum viride var. *virescens* 26
Corallorhiza
   maculata 28
   odontorhiza 29
   striata 30
   trifida 31
Coralroot
   Autumn (Late) 29
   Early (Northern) 31
   Spotted 28
   Striped 30
Cypripedium
   acaule 33
   arietinum 34
   calceolus 35
   candidum 37
   parviflorum 36
   pubescens 35
   reginae 38
Dinner Plate Orchid 86
Dragon's Mouth 20
European Common Twayblade 69

Epipactis
   decipiens (*Goodyera oblongifolia*) 60
   helleborine 40
   repens (*Goodyera repens*) 62
   tesselata (*Goodyera tesselata*) 63
   willdenovii (*Goodyera pubescens*) 61
Fairy Slipper 24
Fen Orchid 65
Fringed Orchid (Orchis)
   Prairie (Prairie White) 83
   Ragged 82
   Small Purple 87
   White 76
Frog Orchid 26
Galearis spectabilis 42
Goldcrest 89
Goodyera
   decipiens (*G. oblongifolia*) 60
   menziesii (*G. oblongifolia*) 60
   oblongifolia 60
   ophioides (*G. repens*) 62
   pubescens 61
   repens var. *ophioides* 62
   tesselata 63
Grass Pink 22
Green Woodland Orchis 77
Habenaria
   blephariglottis (*Platanthera blephariglottis*) 76
   bracteata (*Coeloglossum viride*) 26
   clavellata (*Platanthera clavellata*) 77
   dilatata (*P. dilatata*) 78
   flava (*P. flava*) 79
   hookeri (*P. hookeri*) 80
   hyperborea (*P. hyperborea*) 81
   lacera (*P. lacera*) 82
   leucophaea (*P. leucophaea*) 83
   macrophylla (*P. orbiculata* var. *macro:*) 86
   obtusata (*P. obtusata*) 84
   orbiculata (*P. orbiculata*) 85
   psycodes (*P. psycodes*) 87
   unalascensis (*Piperia unalascensis*) 74
   viridis (*Coeloglossum viride*) 26
Heart Leaved Twayblade 68
Helleborine 40

Hooker's Orchid 80
Ladies' Tresses
   Case's 91
   Great Plains (Prairie)..95
   Hooded...96
   Nodding..92
   Shining (Wide Leaved) 94
   Slender (Northern Slender) 93
Lady's Slipper
   Pink (Stemless) 33
   Ram's Head 34
   Showy (Queen) 38
   Small White...37
   Large Yellow 35
   Small Yellow 36
Large Round Leaved Orchid 86
Liparis loeselii 65
Listera
   convallarioides...67
   cordata 68
   ovata...69
Loesel's Twayblade 65
Long Bracted Green Orchid 26
Malaxis
   bayardi (*M. unifolia*)..72
   brachypoda (*M. monophyllos*) 71
   monophyllos var. *brachypoda* 71
   unifolia 72
Moccasin Flower (Pink)..33
One Leaf Rein Orchid 84
Orchis
   rotundifolia (*Amerorchis rotundifolia*)..............16
   spectabilis (*Galearis spectabilis*).....................42
Piperia unalascensis 74
Platanthera
   aquilonis..81
   blephariglottis..76
   clavellata...77
   dilatata 78
   flava...79
   hookeri 80
   huronensis 81
   hyperborea 81
   lacera 82
   leucophaea 83
   obtusata...84
   orbiculata 85
   macrophylla 86
   psycodes..87

Pogonia ophioglossoides.......................................89
Putty Root 18
Queen Lady's Slipper...38
Rattlesnake Plantain
   Checkered 63
   Downy 61
   Lesser (Dwarf) 62
   Menzies' (Green Leaved, Giant) 60
Rein Orchids
   Blunt Leaf Rein Orchid....................................84
   Club Spur Orchid 77
   Dinner Plate Orchid 86
   Green Woodland Orchis 77
   Hooker's Orchid...80
   Large Round Leaved Orchid 86
   One Leaf Rein Orchid 84
   Prairie Fringed Orchid 83
   Ragged Fringed Orchid....................................82
   Round Leaved Orchid 85
   Small Purple Fringed Orchid 87
   Tall Northern Green Orchid 81
   Tall White Bog Orchid (Bog Candles).............78
   Tubercled Orchid 79
   White Fringed Orchis.......................................76
Rose Pogonia 89
Round Leaf Orchid 85
Showy Orchis 42
Small Round Leaved Orchis 16
Snake Mouth 89
Spiranthes
   casei 91
   cernua 92
   gracilis (*S. lacera*)..93
   lacera 93
   lucida..94
   magnicamporum 95
   romanzoffiana 96
Swamp Pink 20
Tall Leafy Green Orchid 81
Tall White Bog Orchid 78
Tubercled Orchid 79
Twayblades
   Broad Lipped (Broad Leaved) 67
   European Common 69
   Heart Leaved 68
   Loesel's (Bog)...65

NOTES